CRAFTERNOON

CRAFTE

RNOON

A Guide to Getting Artsy and Crafty with Your Friends All Year Long

maura madden

illustrated by leela corman

SIMON SPOTLIGHT ENTERTAINMENT

New York   London   Toronto   Sydney

Simon Spotlight Entertainment
A Division of Simon & Schuster, Inc.
1230 Avenue of the Americas
New York, NY 10020
Text copyright © 2008 by Maura Madden
Illustrations copyright © 2008 by Leela Corman

First Simon Spotlight Entertainment trade paperback edition October 2008

SIMON SPOTLIGHT ENTERTAINMENT and colophon are trademarks
of Simon & Schuster, Inc.

For information about special discounts for bulk purchases,
please contact Simon & Schuster Special Sales at 1-800-456-6798
or business@simonandschuster.com

Designed by Jane Archer/www.psbella.com
Sample craft projects on pages 79, 89, 115, and 193 by Maura Madden;
pages 7, 23, 45, 63, and 103 by Jane Archer;
pages 143 and 171 by Yaffa Jaskoll; and page 193 by M. Pamela Madden

Manufactured in the United States of America

10   9   8   7   6   5   4   3   2   1

Library of Congress Cataloging-in-Publication Data

Madden, Maura, 1975-
    Crafternoon : a guide to getting artsy and crafty with your friends
all year long / Maura Madden ; illustrated by Leela Corman. — 1st ed.
        p. cm.
    Includes bibliographical references and index.
    ISBN-13: 978-1-4169-5471-2 (pbk. : alk. paper)
    ISBN-10:   1-4169-5471-6 (pbk. : alk. paper)
    1. Handicraft. 2. Seasons in art. I. Title.
TT157.M337 2008
745.5—dc22
                                                            2008013684

for **my mother**, the craftiest lady I know

ACKNOWLEDGMENTS

Massive thanks to my mom, my dad, and my brother for your constant love and support. To Rufus Tureen, for every single thing: You are my perfect friend. To my grandmothers, who are always in my heart. To Emilie Stewart, a great friend and a tremendous literary agent: This book wouldn't exist without you. To Team Crafternoon at Simon Spotlight Entertainment, especially my wonderful editor, Emily Westlake; the publisher, Jen Bergstrom; the editorial director, Tricia Boczkowski; the phenomenal interior designers, Jane Archer and Nancy Singer; the managing editors, Sally Franklin and David Logsdon; the meticulous copy editor, Diane Sinitsky; the production editor, Nancy Tonik; the publicist, Kristin Dwyer; and the cover designer, Michael Nagin. To my illustrator, Leela Corman, whose gorgeous pictures are worth a thousand words. To Christine Poreba, my best friend in the whole world: Your friendship and editing skills are invaluable, lady. To all the Crafternooners, past and present, whose creativity and enthusiasm turned a valentine-making party into a way of life. Special thanks go out to all the folks who hosted a Crafternoon in their homes: Jen Posner, Beverlie Leano, Christine Poreba, Mitch Goldman, Joel Tompkins, Erika Rauer, Lori Bower, Emilie Stewart, Jesse Hartman, and Mo Pitkin's House of Satisfaction. To my Crafternoon guinea pigs: Cat Warner, Gabe Roth, Samara Kupferberg, and Tali Woodward: You're kind, patient people. To Shira Kronzon, for the fantastic author photo. To everyone at Comedy Central: You are the heroes! To the kids of Killing My Lobster, 1998–2002: Sweet boy-girl party! To Sabrina Gschwandtner, for the inspiration, and Cassandra Thoreson, for the quilting instruction. To all the folks who gave advice or lent an ear, especially Maria Alcon, Michele Ganeless, Kate Grodd, Jessi Klein, Miriam Latzer, Christina Lee, Julie Miller, Chris Patch, Peter Risafi, Becky Rothbaum, and Susan Tureen. And thanks to all the friends and family who have made my life happier, healthier, and craftier.

CONTENTS

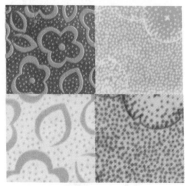

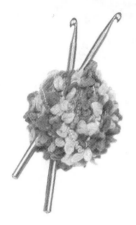

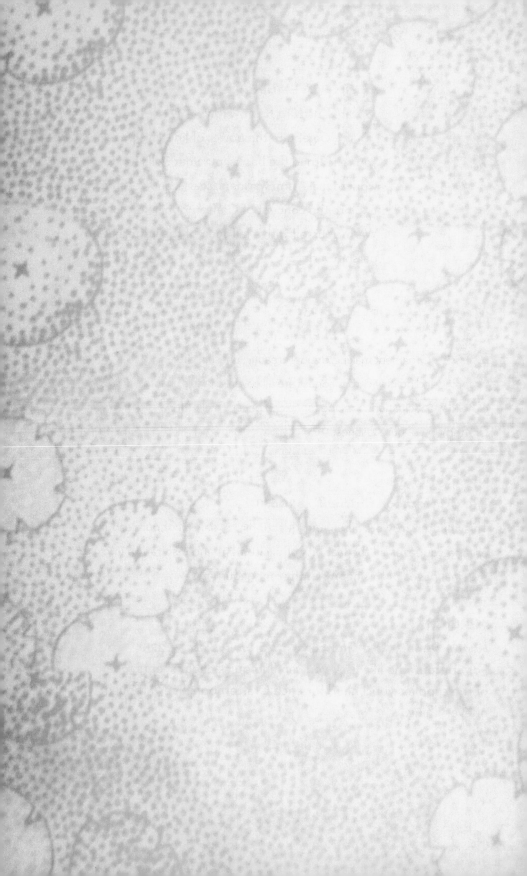

the sweet history and philosophy of

CRAFTERNOON

This is the story of Crafternoon. Once upon a time in February 2002, I was living in San Francisco, the beautiful city by the sea. By day, I worked at a nonprofit, and by night, I spent most of my time putting on sketch comedy shows with my friends. We were a creative and dynamic group of folks devoted to making funny performances. That month we were putting up a new show, and in honor of this occasion, my mom was coming for a visit. And whenever my mom came for a visit, we always had a rocking good time.

Since my mom was flying all the way from New York to California to show her love for me, I wanted to show some love in return, so I decided to throw her a party. But my mom is not the sort of mom who does keg-stands. More power to those moms, I suppose, but my mom's a chiller. So I had to figure out what type of party my mom would dig the most.

Conveniently enough, my mom and I are both huge fans of the day of St. Valentine. You can call it a Hallmark holiday until the cows come home, but as far as my mom and I are concerned, Valentine's Day rules the school. Especially when you show your love with something handmade. Do you see where I'm going with this? I was thinking party, then I was thinking valentines, then, boom, I was thinking: Valentine-Making Party.

See, my mom loves to craft. In fact, "She's Crafty" by The Beastie Boys is actually dedicated to her. Okay, I'm lying about that, but she is an outrageously crafty lady. The lady knits, she crochets, she sews, she embroiders, she smocks, she weaves, she draws, she collages, she etceteras, etceteras, etceteras. She rocks craft! My mom knows how much people value things that are made by hand, and she just so happens to be great at making those things. She has always believed in the importance of a handknit baby sweater or a needlepoint pillow. She made pot holders for our entire comedy group as a token of her love. Yes, pot holders—she can do anything!

When I was a kid, my mother was always coming up with different crafts for my brother and me to do, whatever the season. And this made my house a popular place to visit. Recently, I've run into some friends that I haven't seen since grade school. Time and again, they wax poetic about a gingerbread house we decorated together or some T-shirts we designed at my house. My mom always came up with interesting projects to keep us stimulated, and decades later, people still remember.

So in February 2002, I hosted a little party. And though this gathering was not yet dubbed Crafternoon, it was a Crafternoon all the same. My friends and my mom gathered at my house, then we sewed and we cut and we drew our way to creating handmade displays of old-fashioned romance. We were armed with paper of many colors, as well as glitter and fake fur and old magazines and glue sticks and crayons and markers. We feasted on cupcakes, cookies, finger sandwiches, and pots of tea. The scissors were passed all around, the needles were threaded through fabric, and the fun spilled everywhere.

It was more awesome than I could have imagined. What I thought would just be a cool little party where my mom could hang out with my friends turned out to be something else as well. For as my friends crafted fuzzy wristlets and paper hearts and insane medallions to express their affection, the love of craft was re-kindled inside me.

I carried this love cross-country in September of 2002 when I moved from California back to New York City. I was born and raised in New York City, so it was a homecoming journey. Yes, I crossed this big country called America, knitting for hours on end as my then boyfriend drove us east. His days and days of driving earned him my very first knit project—a scarf of many colors filled with tons of love.

I settled in Brooklyn, and the transition was hard at first. But I was now just a borough away from my family, so my mom and I could have quality time whenever we liked. Sharing an apartment with my best friend in the world and rediscovering old friends who had been far away for so long helped a lot. Soon enough, I added to the friend stew with some new buds, then before I knew it, it was time to throw another Valentine-Making Party.

So in February 2003, I gathered my New York friends and my mom for an afternoon of cupcakes and craft. I didn't even consider doing it without my mom—her presence at the first party was a huge part of what had made it so fun. My New York friends love her, too. In New York, as in San Francisco, it seems that so many people are living far from their families. Everyone likes to have my mom around to give crafty advice or even just to add spice to conversations. She is patient and kind with her instructions, and she makes everyone feel at home. And that's what Crafternoon is really all about.

But the boyfriend and I had broken up, so I didn't much feel like watching boys and girls make lovey-dovey eyes at each other while they crafted their homemade valentines. So I made it an all-girls party, and it was a huge success. At the end of this party, we came to a decision—it was too fun to wait a whole year to do again. This had to become a regular gathering. Boys might even be allowed. And so it was born, the afternoon of craft, or what has come to be known as Crafternoon.

Crafternoon speaks to that space inside all of us that wants to make things and share the things we make with those we love. To some people in the world of fancy craft, the things we make may seem weird or unsophisticated, but that doesn't matter. Crafternoon is all about being around friends who support your work, who encourage your growing craftiness, and who inspire and get inspired by you. Crafternoon is about getting back to the roots of crafting. It's about getting pleasure out of the process as much as the product. It's about making room for the input of other crafters and allowing yourself to be open to new ideas. It's about the contentment you feel when you are surrounded by happily crafting friends, friends who can see the beauty in imperfection, the pleasure of happy mistakes. Your inspiration can come from out of the blue or by watching someone making something extraordinary out of something that looked ordinary moments ago. Crafternoon has the feeling of craft time in preschool, when crafting is all about the joy of playing with materials and looking at other people's art and trying to make yours as big as your imagination. In a community engaged in the process of making, it is easy to find something newly beautiful. And the bonus is, you wind up with something special to take home and treasure or give away to be treasured by another. Crafternoon is about making what you want, how you want it, to the best of your ability. And even if you may not think of yourself as a rock star of creativity, it's there inside you. At Crafternoon, you are a CraftStar.

In San Francisco, I had been lucky to be surrounded by friends who were always making things—comedy shows and music and videos and T-shirts and jokes. Though I have just as many wonderful, creative friends in New York, lives often move in a million different rapidly changing orbits in this big apple of a city. And it can be hard to bring people together no matter where you live. Crafternoon is the thing that pulls people in from every part of my life, gathers them in one place for a few hours, and teaches them how to stitch something. And that's no small thing.

Plus, Crafternoon is a neutral ground where different social circles seamlessly come together. There is no pressure to make romantic connections; there is no assumption that any business deals will be made. All that is to be expected to come of a good Crafternoon is a warm feeling and maybe something handmade. And unlike other gatherings that can be divided by generations, Crafternoon has room for people of all ages. Because it's not just my mom who makes the Crafternoon circle expand. It's my friend Marie and her young daughter Madeline, and it's Lucas, a boy I used to babysit, and his mom, Winona. It's the younger sister of my high school friend who is now in high school herself. And it's the other moms and aunts and friends of Mom's who make the event a more textured and therefore more joyful affair. For the nonparents of my age group, intergenerational interaction is predominantly relegated to family events, but Crafternoon builds a community that promotes generational inclusiveness. I think of knitting circles and quilting bees and fishermen gathering to mend their nets—groups gathering to support each other through crafts.

Craft is certainly making a comeback in the mainstream, but all too often, the preached and published craft is mostly about perfection. The magazines and television shows demonstrate crafts that seem obsessed with being neat and well executed. But that's not what Crafternoon is about. I am not a perfect crafter, nor do I care to be. I am an enthusiastic crafter, a crafter who learns at my own pace, a crafter who will not be intimidated by the expectations of others. I craft because it makes me happy and because I seek to make others happy through my craft. It's not a competition for me. I am not "good" at drawing, and my sewing is sloppy. I don't have the patience to embroider something without it looking messy, I can't string little beads to save my life, and I cannot follow a knitting pattern. I like the possibilities that open up to someone when she approaches a craft without limitations. But I am always open to learning and am inspired by people whose skills vary from mine.

Take quilting. I'll tell you how to do all sorts of quilting projects, but I'm not going to tell you how to trim. Any instructions that involve 45-degree angles are more than either you or I bargained for. Making an entire quilt is just way too complicated for me to explain in one chapter. That's why I'm giving you a taste, a sampler, if you will, of what each craft has to offer. After all, this book is about projects that can be done or almost totally done in one afternoon. The book isn't called CrafterWeek. That's the sequel, baby.

Craft can be practiced by anyone, regardless of the skill or artistry that has come to be demanded by those who preach craft. Like a good meal, a good Crafternoon shouldn't need much—a few quality ingredients, a couple of good friends, and a little bit of creativity. So turn the page and let's get started on the journey of Crafternoon!

CHAPTER ONE

JANUARY

KNOTTY OR NICE

It's January, you've got bills to pay and gifts to return. The holiday hubbub has a way of draining every last ounce of energy out of a person. If you're a confirmed crafter, you probably spent most of November and nearly all of December crafting till your hands hurt. And even if you're not a crafter, you probably had to wrap the heck out of some presents. Holidays mean ribbon wrangling and paper folding, all with the goal of dazzling your gifts' recipients. Quite frankly, you might feel a little bit sick of crafty activities. But fear not, gentle crafter! The remedy for your crafting fatigue is right around the corner. You're going to start the year off on the right foot, and that foot is Crafternoon!

Each new year is filled with the promise of endless possibilities. It's tradition to make resolutions, and it's an even bigger tradition to break them. But this year is going to be different—this year is The Year of the Crafternoon. And this is one resolution you will stick to like macaroni on construction paper. You want to break out of the postholiday funk that's hanging over you like a cartoon cloud. You have the urge to socialize, but the thought of wearing your little black dress makes you woozy. You want to play hostess to your friends, but you refuse to stuff another little pig into a little dough blanket. Well, you've come to the right place—you've come to Crafternoon country.

The first Crafternoon of the year should be something new and exciting. It shouldn't require a lot of expensive materials, because most of us have empty pockets come January. So you're looking for an exotic but low-cost craft. Let's assume that some of your friends have been knitting up a storm in preholiday prep. After all, it seems that the handknit scarf has become the fruitcake of our generation. It may not be as unwelcome, but it's becoming as ubiquitous. But how many of your friends have been *knotting* up a storm? Unless you reside on Gilligan's Island or surround yourself with nautical mates, chances are a Knotting Crafternoon will be just the sort of exotic, low-budget craft to kick off your Crafter Year!

Since I'd decided on knotting as my New Year's kickoff craft, I needed to find someone to lead me and my fellow crafters to knotting glory. My friend Chris's dad is a sailor, and he practices the art of knotting every day as he sails the Hudson River. This seemed like an alignment of the craft stars, and I got very, very excited. I wanted to host the knotting Crafternoon right away with Chris's dad at the helm. But sailors are married to the sea. Turns out you can't just hop off the boat for a few hours. His two-month tour had just begun when I thought of the knotting idea, so he wasn't available to lead the knotting brigade. But a friend of a friend who was practiced in the art offered to lend his skills to the crafty cause, and so my Knotting Crafternoon idea was saved.

As a side note, knotting struck me as the sort of craft that appeals to the menfolk and the womenfolk alike. I'm not trying to be sexist or sexy, I'm just saying that seamen have been knotting for centuries now. It's a macho, dude-approved sort of craft, if you're looking at it through that sort of lens. Me, I think *all* crafts appeal equally to dudes and to ladies. But in my experience, the ladies often hop on the crafting trends faster than the dudes. I aim to change that, one crafty dude at a time, and where better to start than with some extreme knotting!

GET THE WORD OUT AND SET UP YOUR SPACE

Get people in seats with a fun email invite. This is the email I sent to entice my crafters to tie themselves into knots for craft's sake:

> *Boys and girls who love to craft, this email is for you! This Satur-day at 2 p.m., Crafternoon is the place to be. The theme? Why, it's Knots and Whatnot!*
>
> *Why Knots? Well, a crafter on the list wanted some lessons on knotting, and I thought that sounded rad! So he found us a sur-prise guest to teach the ways of the ropes, sailor style. Knowing how to make good knots is a practical art! Ever tie furniture to a car or make a rope swing? If you've got the knot know-how, then, oh, how fun your days of tying can become! Bring a bit of the ropes and learn them! And if anyone knows macramé, well then, show us how!*
>
> *Why Whatnot? Well, Whatnot is what you can do if you feel the crafting fever but are allergic to rope. Bring any craft project you like, and you can work on it in the company of friends. As always, there will be the Mother Crafter (my mom) on hand to answer your craft questions.*

I do hope I might see you there! Please be encouraged to bring a treat along to share, a beverage or a cake or some savory delights. Savory treats are extra-especially welcome!

xoxo,

Maura

This email worked like a charm, especially with the menfolk. I think it was the comment about tying furniture to a car. Dudes love to tie furniture to cars. It's a primal instinct, the need to tie big things to vehicles. It worked like an invitational charm. In fact, the turnout for my Knotty Crafternoon was small but dude-heavy. We had fewer than ten people in attendance, and half of those people were dudes. I like that in a Crafternoon. Having a solid showing of dudes is a good sign that you've chosen a craft with a wide appeal. Again, I'm not saying that ladies craft more than dudes, I'm just saying that nine times out of ten, more ladies show up for my Crafternoon than dudes. So it's cool when you find a craft that evens the playing field.

That Crafternoon was a mix of old friends and new ones. Crafternoon has a way of making that happen. Myra, who has been my friend since first grade, was on spring break from her job as a college photography professor, so she joined the knotty crew. Gideon, a college friend who is a civil rights lawyer, showed up. It was an honor to know that he was taking time out of his packed schedule to sit down and tie some knots with us. And Ruben, the leader of the pack, was a guy I'd never met before. But he came highly recommended by Paul, an artist who came along, too. And of course, my mom was in attendance. Of all of the Crafternoons I've hosted, I think she's missed only one. She is definitely the number one fan of Crafternoon. It was an eclectic and inspiring group of crafters, and I wouldn't have it any other way.

KNOTTY SUPPLIES

As far as materials go, I personally love a simple length of white rope. Nevertheless, I was pleased when Ruben, our craft leader, brought along a coil of black rope. To get your supplies, head to your local hardware store and grab some rope of various widths and colors and materials. I think that cotton rope is the way to go when you're crafting. I like the way it looks, and I like the way it feels when you're getting your craft on. I mean, rappelling down a rock face might require a rope built to endure extreme elements, but pretty cotton rope accessories won't be used to save you from a 100-foot drop. At least I hope they won't. If you have a tendency to find yourself in MacGyver-esque situations, go ahead and choose a synthetic rope to craft with. I don't want you cursing my name as you hang from a cliff by your swiftly fraying Monkey's Fist necklace. Choose the synthetic stuff if your life resembles a spy movie. That way you'll be covering your butt whether you're strolling on the beach collecting shells or on top of a skyscraper saving a dude in distress.

TREAT OF THE 'NOON:
Hot Dip! An Artichoke Appetizer

Small jar of artichoke hearts marinated in oil and herbs
Juice of 1 lemon
½ cup grated Parmesan cheese
¼ cup mayo

Preheat the oven to 350°F. Take the artichoke hearts out of the jar and chop them, reserving the liquid. In a bowl, mix the artichokes with all of the other ingredients. Transfer to an oven-safe container, then bake until bubbling. Serve with fresh bread or pita chips.

INTERIOR DESIGN:
UNDERWATER FANTASY CRAFT PROM

Most Crafternoons, I don't do a lot to prepare aside from clean-ing up. Sometimes that qualifies as doing a lot. Scratch that—most of the time it qualifies as a lot. I try to keep the house clean, but it's pretty hard to keep up when there are so many things that are way more fun than cleaning. So pre-Crafternoon the house gets a thorough cleanup, I throw a nice bunch of flowers in a vase, and boom, the decorating is done. But if you're feeling decorative, you could do up your place with some nautical décor. I'm all for an under-the-sea theme, and it's easy enough to hang colored ribbons from the ceiling and attach construction-paper fish, fishhooks, and anchors from the ends. Simply start with a sketch of a fish, a fishhook, or an anchor.

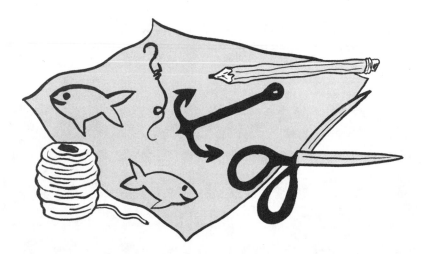

Using tracing paper, trace the image onto it, then cut the image out. Once you've got your cutout, you can use it as a pattern to cut multiple fish or anchors out of paper and hang them all around. The more colorful and shiny the paper and ribbons, the more festive and underwateresque your home will be.

CRAFTERNOON INTERLUDE: *The Frugal Crafter*

Back in the day, I had a strict policy on spending: I didn't spend more than $25 on a Crafternoon. These days, I spend a little more cash if I'm feeling the fever, but it's not a necessity. And that is one of the joys of Crafternoon—you can have an awesome party without spending a wad of cash. That's part of the reason I started throwing Crafternoons in the first place— I wanted to play hostess to my friends, but I seemed to be constantly strapped for cash. By hosting a daytime party that didn't have booze on the menu, I could play hostess on a regular basis without defaulting on my student loans. I spent a few bucks on supplies, bought some snacks and drinks, picked up a small bouquet of flowers, and I was all set.

Even $25 may be more than some Crafternoon hosts need or want to spend. If you can't spend anything at all, you can still throw a Crafternoon. Search your cupboards for snack-making materials—flour, sugar, oatmeal, and oil. If you're willing to bake something, you can make a snack that costs almost nothing. Flip through your favorite cookbook or look online for recipes that you can make with things you already have. Provide a cheap beverage by making black or herbal iced tea or even coffee. And then dig up every magazine and piece of scrap paper you've been hoarding and make them into a big pile of craft supplies. Tell folks to bring something to add to the supply pile and to come locked and loaded with their own scissors and glue sticks. Then you'll be ready to go. That's what I like to call the Crafternoon Stone Soup effect. Stone what? Oh, come on now, you remember that old folk tale about the hungry travelers, don't you? No? Then cozy up to the fire and give it a listen:

A small group of hungry travelers stop in a village for the night. They bring out a large cauldron, fill it with water, and add a stone. They light a fire and start the cauldron boiling. The villagers begin to come around, asking what's in the big pot. The travelers tell them they are making stone soup. The villagers are intrigued. "Oh, yes, this is some tasty soup," the travelers exclaim. "Though it would be even better if only we had a few carrots!" The villagers start donating additions to the stone soup—one potato here, one carrot there, some oregano, a chicken, whatever they have handy. Before you know it, the hungry travelers and the whole village are able to eat well from this big, nutritious pot of "stone" soup. And that's the concept of Crafternoon—you start with something small, but as a group, you end up with something huge.

KNOT ADVICE

While knotting is totally satisfying when you're getting it right, it can be quite frustrating when you are getting it wrong. When I had my knotting Crafternoon, our instructor was very patient. He really took his time explaining how to complete each step on a given knot and gave extra help when we needed it. I had some trouble with some of the knots, but he was there to check on the positioning of my hands and explain what was going wrong. I picked up on a few of the knots throughout the afternoon and felt quite accomplished by the end of the day. But going back to those knots after some time had passed, I felt completely at a loss. A few weeks after my Knotting Crafternoon, I decided to follow some instructions on the Internet and found myself sitting in front of the computer for an hour, desperately trying to understand why the monkey's fist wasn't forming the way it did in the picture. Sometimes you're crafting something and it just doesn't click, and that can feel really bad. But it doesn't have to. And you need to realize that knotting is a craft that requires a lot of focus and patience. When you are working down a knot, tightening it so that it forms the knot in the picture, it is pretty easy for it to go wrong, especially on your first try. Don't give up. Untie the rope and try again. Or if you've created a tangled monster of a knot that's not worth untying, just get a new length of rope and start knotting again. Take your time. Stare at the instructions. And above all, just focus, focus, focus.

But fear not! In the margin of an old book by George Russell Shaw called *Knots: Useful and Ornamental,* I found a handwritten note. Describing the illustration of a bowline knot, someone had written, "Snake goes through lake around tree and then bites himself." Reading that childlike description reminded me that there are so many different ways to process the same information. Looking at certain knotting illustrations, the ones with the arrows going in a million directions and the complicated angles, my brain starts freaking out and yelling, "Math! Math! Math!" Turns out I'm not the first person to make this freaked-out connection. In fact, mathematicians have a whole theory based on this craft—it's called Knot Theory. Where one person sees a snake, another person sees a formula. So try to wrap the knots around your brain one way or another. And if you try all of those things and it still doesn't work, take a break. Laugh it off. You'll get it. You just need some time away from it. Don't give up completely. Give it some time, and then start knotting again. You'll be glad you didn't give up the ghost.

It's also important to remember that while other Crafternoons will result in final products, the Knotty 'Noon is more about the process. And in a season that's marked by returns, exchanges, and overwhelmingly full closets, it's nice to learn a craft whose tangible results get stored in your brain, not in a dresser drawer. You have the option to make things that you can keep forever, but you may simply choose to take in the techniques.

HOW TO TEACH PEOPLE:
Knowledge Plus Patience
Plus Smiles Equals Good Teachin'

Before we get down to business with our first project, we have yet another lesson to learn about staging a successful Crafternoon: When you are the expert at a Crafternoon, it's your job to share your crafty knowledge with your friends. But sharing isn't enough—you need to be a Good Teacher. Don't worry, you don't have to attend a three-hour class in a church basement to become a Good Teacher. Just keep these simple facts in mind: A Good Teacher (or GT for short) explains things slowly and clearly. A GT takes questions and answers them thoughtfully. A GT encourages his or her students, and never, ever judges them. And a GT strives always to be kind and compassionate. A Good Teacher doesn't just blah blah blah at people or bulldoze over inquiries or stare blankly at you while you attempt something new. And a Good Teacher is never, ever mean.

At one Crafternoon, I had a firsthand experience with a Bad Teacher (or BT for short). For this 'noon, I had a few experts on hand teaching the Craft o' the Day. (To protect the identity of both the victim and the perp, I can't tell you which craft. Ha-ha, witchcraft!) Anywho, one of our teachers was very skilled in the chosen craft but not nearly as skilled in the teaching department. She had to leave halfway through the Crafternoon, and after she left, one of her students sidled up to me. In a bashful half-whisper, the student asked if someone else could teach her the craft. Turns out she hadn't learned much because her teacher had made learning a completely stressful experience. She had hurriedly explained the how-tos, rushing her student through every step. In this high-speed atmosphere, the student felt that there wasn't time for questions. When the explanation was over, the BT had thrown the tools at the newbie crafter and told her to try her hand at this brand-new craft. She stared at the student while she stopped and started, and then she got frustrated when her pupil didn't get things right. She even snatched the student's craft project away from her a few times in a puff of exasperation. If the gentlemen of Van Halen were to rewrite their song and dedicate it to her, they'd call it "Cold for Teacher (and Her Teaching Methodology)."

Now, to be fair to the teacher, she was trying to be helpful. She could have just sat to the side and done her own crafting, but she offered to share her knowledge. She just didn't know how to share it. It can be very hard to teach—there's often a gap between what we know and how we can communicate that knowledge. So remind yourself of the attributes of the Good Teacher: Take your time, answer questions, offer encouragement, and be kind. Above all, remind yourself how it feels to be a student. With patience and sensitivity, you can guide your crafters through any new task.

So whatever happened to our shell-shocked little newbie? I put her in the care of my dear momma, who swiftly administered a patient crafting lesson and lots of big smiles. Smiles go a long way, in craft as in life, so feel free to add them to your next lesson plan.

KNOT PROJECT NUMBER ONE:

DON'T FEAR THE REEF KNOT

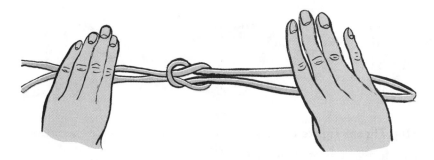

While there are plenty of crazy knots in this world, some of the best are also the simplest. This knot will introduce you to the joys of entanglement without turning your stomach into, ahem, *knots*.

Supplies: *Rope, scissors*

Optional: *Two scarves*

Step One: *Double U.* Using two ropes of the same length (approximately three feet each), make two U-shaped loops on a tabletop. Then turn the U's so they are lying sideways with the openings facing each other, as shown.

Step Two: *Interlocking.* Pull the open ends of the loops toward the closed sides of the opposite loop, making an overlapped circle.

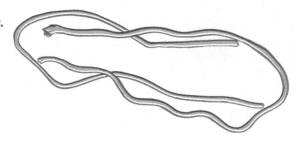

Feed the open rope ends under the arc on the left side and over the arc on the right side, as shown.

Step Three: *Tighten.* Pull on the ends of both ropes at the same time to tighten. Voilà! You've got a great knot.

You can also use this knot to make a really cool belt. First, look for two scarves of approximately the same length. I chose two flower-patterned scarves that have an older Eastern European Lady vibe going on. Roll each scarf into a long tube. Follow the steps for making the Reef Knot, using the scarves instead of the rope. The Reef Knot is a great design. You can secure the belt at the back with small overhand knots. This belt makes any outfit look more interesting and sophisticated.

By no means should you use these knots to secure your furniture, your dog, or your boat loaded with furniture captained by your dog. I am (k)not a knot expert—I'm a novice knotter. Get yourself to a salty sea dog or a scoutmaster who can literally show you the ropes if someone's life depends upon your knots. But you can knot your way to some crafty good times with the above instructions, and crafty good times are worth their weight in gold.

KNOT PROJECT NUMBER TWO:
FIGURE EIGHT KNOT

The Figure Eight is a good knot to make. How does it get its name, you ask? Well, when you've looped it correctly before tightening it, it looks exactly like a figure eight. Yeah, they're pretty creative, those knot namers. Here's how you make that special knot your very own.

Supplies
Rope, scissors

Step One: *First turn.* Lay the rope out so it looks like an unfinished figure eight laying on its side, as shown.

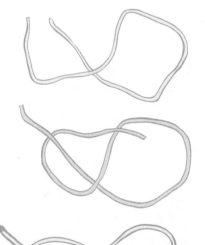

Step Two: *Second turn.* Now take the overlapping end of rope and feed it up and under the other end of rope, and then drag it to the right and over the closed part of the loop, as shown.

Then feed that end through the bottom right edge of that loop, as shown.

Now pull it tighter so that it really looks like a figure eight, as shown.

Step Three: *Tighten.* Pulling gently from both sides, completely tighten the knot. You will get a simple and pretty knot in the center of your rope.

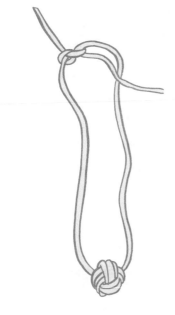

KNOT PROJECT NUMBER THREE:
MONKEY'S FIST NECKLACE

Big, bold medallions are making a comeback. But while silver or gold will set you back a bundle, a rope rendition won't cost you more than a fiver. So focus your attention on the ways of the line, and we'll have you sporting a sophisticated shout-out to the seafaring life in no time.

Supplies
Rope, scissors

Optional: Cork, jewelry wire, jewelry pliers

Step One: *First rotation.*
Take a nine-foot length of rope and fold it in half. Slide your submissive hand under the fold. Taking the back piece of the rope, loop it up and around your fingers three times. Note: you will use the same number of loops at each step.

Step Two: *Second rotation.*
Feed the active, or bitter, end of the rope to the left through the first set of loops. Bring it through the loops and around to the front of your hand.

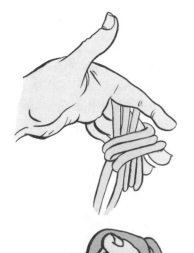

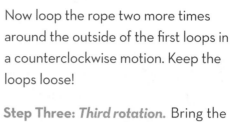

Now loop the rope two more times around the outside of the first loops in a counterclockwise motion. Keep the loops loose!

Step Three: *Third rotation.* Bring the rope up and around the second set of turns, circling them three times. These loops will wrap around the outside of the second set of turns but remain inside the first set of turns. Remember, you don't need to keep the loops wrapped tightly around your fingers. As it gets too tight, slide it off toward your fingers. You can work the knot as you hold it on at the edge of your hand.

Step Four: *Tighten.*
Feed a small ball or knot of rope, or half of a cork, into the center-most part of the loops. Carefully tighten the "fist" around the ball until it is completely tight.

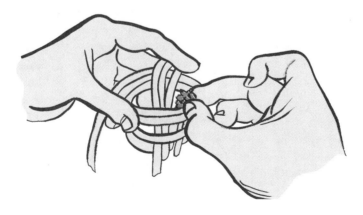

For more visual texture, choose a core that is a different color from the larger knot—it will be peek out from behind the fist and say hello.

Step Five: *Close the circle.* If you are going to leave your rope necklace long, you can create a clasp at the end of your rope with jeweler's wire for a simple, complete look. If you think you might want to wear it long sometimes and short at others, then leave it unfinished so you can tie it to different sizes at different times.

I hope that monkey's fist didn't leave you at the end of your rope, 'cause ready or knot, you've just completed your very first Crafternoon!

CHAPTER TWO

FEBRUARY

LOVE IN THE CRAFTERNOON

Who chose February to be the month of love? In my part of the world, February is the coldest and dreariest month on the calendar. It's more pleasant to be indoors than outdoors, which certainly makes for more quality time with preexisting loved ones, but it's not exactly a time of new romance. February in the Northeast is a bleak time, marked by layers of protective clothing and the onslaught of dry, flaky skin. The magic of the holiday season has worn off, and most folks are weary from battling the winter for a few solid months. No one is walking down the street checking each other out in February. Okay,

maybe in Rio, but not in the Northeast Corridor of the United States. In these parts, everyone seems to resemble a walking marshmallow. Marshmallows are delicious, but you're not going to stop one on the street to get their number.

But it turns out that February has long been a month of fertility rituals, dating back even farther than the era of the famed St. Valentine. As with so many of our holiday celebrations, the ancient tradition has been transformed into something we modern creatures can embrace. To get the blood pumping deep in the heart of winter, we purchase boxes filled with candy, exchange cards and flowers, and eat dinner by candlelight. And then everyone has a sugar headache the next morning.

For loads of people, Valentine's Day is just an obligation. They find no joy in buying overpriced roses. They take no pleasure in getting an 11 p.m. dinner reservation. Their paper-doily hearts aren't in it, but they feel that they must participate in the festivities or they won't hear the end of it. They know they're supposed to show the love, but they're not really feeling it.

Valentine's Day shouldn't be about spending too much money on something you care nothing for. And that's why I believe in a good Love in the Crafternoon. Because shopping for crappy chocolates and expensive flowers can feel like a chore, but making a handmade card equals automatic fun. I've seen plenty of people leave a flower shop with a gorgeous bouquet and a terrible grimace, but I've never seen someone leave a Crafternoon with anything less than a smile.

If you read the introduction to this book, you know that Crafternoon was born out of a valentine-making party. If you didn't read the introduction, go back and read it now. It's funny and inspiring. Go ahead, read it, I'll wait. . . .

Okay, you're back. Valentine making has been a long-standing tradition in my family. My mother has always been a firm believer in the power of a handmade valentine. But when I was a kid, I was frustrated by the handmade-only policy. Sometime around third grade, I wanted to betray our valentine-making tradition. Most of my friends were giving out the kind of valentines that popped out of boxes of 40. For some reason, those personality-less perforated paper products were more appealing to me than the unique little works of art my mom and I would make. My handmade valentines felt quaint. The beautiful doilies and colored paper were too old-fashioned. I wanted to join the 1980s and embrace the pop culture that surrounded me. I longed to hand out the kind of valentines that said, "My mom ran out to the grocery store at the last minute and bought hundreds of these! Happy Valentine's Day!" But my mother held firm and handmade we stayed. And it's true what they say—Mother knows best. Now when I think of those kids with their boxes of perforated pop-culture cards, I think of missed opportunities to craft. Holidays like Valentine's Day were a great reason to take the crafting to the next level!

GET THE WORD OUT AND SET UP YOUR SPACE

You're set to craft up a storm, but you need to invite your guests along for the ride. Here's my latest Love in the Crafternoon invite email. It'll give you a sense of how to get your guests fired up to attend, and prepared to do so.

> Love in the Crafternoon this Saturday! It's the time of the season for loving. . . .

> St. Valentine's Day is nearly upon us, and I think there's no better way to show your love than to make your loved ones a valentine by hand. Sure, you could run out and buy a shiny store-bought number, showing that you can express the way you feel exactly the same way that 75,000 other people do, but come on, you're more creative than that. Hey, that's why I like you. So this Saturday, at 3 p.m., please join me for Love in the Crafternoon!

Numerous types of paper and glue and scissors and glitter and stickers and fabric and needles and thread and bunnies and moonbeams and crayons and gargoyles will be provided, but please bring some additional materials to share. The more craft materials we have, the better.

Anything that you are inspired to bring along, we will embrace and somebody will use. Old magazines and other things with rad images that can be chopped to pieces are most welcome. And bring on the coffee lids and bottle caps and paper dolls and hazmat tape and pastels. No craft item shall be turned away.

We love it when people bring treats to share. Savory nibbles and sweet munchies will delight the hungry CrafterNation, or bring along a beverage so that we will remain unparched all the Crafternoon long.

The happy crafty madness will begin at 3 p.m. and go until we are completely exhausted by our crafting.

Please RSVP to let me know if you'll be joining the craftiness, and feel free to pass this invitation along to Crafters I have somehow forgotten or am yet to know. We love new Crafters.

In love and craft we trust,

Maura

From the email above, we can garner a substantial amount of information about the Crafternoon to come. Right off the bat, I put the date and time. That's standard invite etiquette, my friend. Next, I told the future crafters what types of materials they are likely to encounter chez me. I always provide a ton of paper to start the day with. I'm not a person who conforms to many rules, but I know that lots of folks like to use red or pink paper to make their special love notes, so I make sure to buy some good-quality red paper from a paper store or print shop. I supplement that standard red stuff with cool origami paper, wrapping paper, instructional manuals, scraps of fabric, and a lot of old magazines. For the old mags, pre-1980 is generally my rule of thumb. With the '80s making a raging comeback, you might make a splash with a sweet issue of *Teen Beat* featuring a young Jason Bateman, *Teen Wolf Too* era. Mmm, Jason Bateman. I'll take a valentine from that guy anytime.

SUPPLIES ARE US

When you're asking people to share supplies, you're also engaging them in the event. And most people like sharing, especially when you promise you'll share something, too. Anyway, having others donate materials multiplies your crafting possibilities. I search all over for cool raw materials, but there's no way I can find every cool thing that's out there. Believe me, I try, but it's just not possible. When your friends and family are also on the prowl for materials, you'll end up with true variety. And that's great for everyone. My mom always spends the month prior to the Valentine-Making Crafternoon in full-on scouting mode. This doesn't mean she's spending loads of money on paper goods; it just means that she's looking out for neat additions to the craft pile. And when she comes across some cool paper or some sweetheart stickers, she's going to buy them. It's like squirreling stuff away for the long winter.

The combinations that come up when you mix and match materials are a million times more interesting than what you'd make if you had just one materials source. At my very first valentine-making party in San Francisco, my friend Debbie brought a ton of fabric along with her. Debbie has a good eye for great textiles. She donated big patches of white fur, shiny red metallic fabric, yards of sequined ribbon, and plenty of needles and thread. And before I knew it, folks were going mad for the fabric valentines. One little posse made furry bracelets for one another, embellishing them with shiny red hearts in the center. I think they even used Velcro—Debbie thought of everything. My mom showed my then boyfriend Peter how to thread a needle and sew a simple stitch. He sat there quietly making me a big stuffed heart medallion, fur on one side, red shiny fabric on the other, and a sequined ribbon chain to hang it from. It was handmade bling, and the perfect 3-D valentine. I put it on the minute I got it.

Two years ago at a New York Crafternoon, someone brought a 1950s illustrated pamphlet of meat cuts. Each meat illustration was accompanied by a description—Tenderloin, Boneless Rump, Standing Rump, etc. I thought that was hilarious and decided to create a concept collage for my fiancé, Rufus, the best guy in the world. I happened upon a picture of a lovely young lass from the same era, posing in a bathing suit. I cut a selection of three prime cuts out of the meat manual and pasted them over her bathing suit, creating the illusion that she was wearing a meat bathing suit and perhaps giving an ironic nod to the idea that a lady in a bath-

TREAT OF THE 'NOON:
Mary Pamela's Butteriest Cookies Ever

½ pound butter, room temperature

½ pound margarine, room temperature

2 cups sugar

2 whole eggs plus 1 egg yolk

5 ½ to 6 cups flour

2 teaspoons baking powder

1 tablespoon vanilla

sprinkles or jimmies (optional)

16 ounces semisweet chocolate morsels (optional)

Cream the butter, margarine, and sugar together in a big bowl. Add the eggs and blend until smooth. In a separate bowl, sift the flour and baking powder together. Gradually add the flour mixture to the butter mixture. Finally, add the vanilla. Cover the bowl and place it in the refrigerator to chill for at least two hours, up to one day in advance of use.

Preheat the oven to 350°F. Turn the chilled dough out onto a floured pastry cloth. Using a rolling pin covered in a cloth sleeve and then floured, roll the dough out to a uniform thickness.

ing suit is often treated like a piece of meat. Using my friend's typewriter, inside I typed the words, "Want a piece of me?" Ha, that still cracks me up.

In the world of party planning, never underestimate the power of pretty food. In honor of the holiday, my mom makes her famously delicious heart-shaped butter cookies. Using a simple heart-shaped cookie cutter, she cuts the cookies, bakes them, then paints half of each heart with melted chocolate and multicolored sprinkles. Arrange these gorgeous cookies on a plate, and you've instantly amped up the decorations. In fact, you can cut the cookies into any holiday shape you desire—cupids, roses, bikinis, whatever makes you think of Valentine's Day. And if you don't feel like doing the additional chocolate painting step, then before you bake those bad boys, give them a dusting of red sprinkles, throw them in the oven, and they are good to go.

Using cookie cutters, cut hearts or other shapes out of the dough. Carefully remove the cookies from the cutters and place them on a baking sheet. Flour the pastry cloth and rolling pin frequently during the rolling-out process so that the dough does not stick. If decorating with sprinkles or jimmies, add decorations. If decorating with chocolate, leave plain. Bake 7-10 minutes based on the first batch. Cookies should be slightly golden when done. Place them on a wire rack to cool.

For chocolate-dipped hearts, melt the chocolate morsels on the stovetop over a diffuser, which is a metal cooking tool that is placed between your stovetop and your saucepan to diffuse the heat so you don't end up with burnt chocolate. Using a metal spatula or butter knife, spread the chocolate on the back and front of one half of each cookie. Dipping doesn't really work—it leaves you with a lumpy cookie. Lay each chocolate-dipped cookie on a baking sheet covered in waxed paper and add multicolored sprinkles. When the sheet is full of cookies, put it in the freezer until the chocolate hardens. Remove from the freezer, then transfer the cookies to a tin or plastic container and refrigerate. Leave refrigerated until time to serve.

J'ADORE DÉCOR

I always turn up the decorating heat for Love in the Crafternoon (I am a sucker for holiday decorations in general). This is another trait passed down to me by my mom. She decorates in little ways all over the house, but the main decorating spot is the front door of my parents' apartment. There's a handmade wreath that hangs on their apartment door, and nearly every month it receives a face-lift. For February, it's Valentine's Day all the way. Handmade fabric heart ornaments hang from the edges of the wreath, while a paper cupid cutout or doily heart is featured in the wreath's center. Red ribbons with little white heart designs are tied in perky bows. It's Valentinetastic! March is the month of the Irish, and with ancestry as an excuse, my mom decorates it to the hilt. She breaks out the green ribbons and the shamrocks. She poses bendable rubber leprechauns. She even has some old Snoopy decoration featuring Peppermint Patty saying, "It's great to be Irish" and Snoopy quipping, "Even if it's just one day a year." Snoopy, you're such a rascal! She changes the decorations every month, and it's pretty adorable. Most New York apartment doors are bare and soulless, but my parents' door is always flowing over with personality.

So, for your Valentine-Making Crafternoon, it wouldn't hurt to make things a little more festive than usual. Inspired by my mother's welcoming door, I made a door decoration for my first New York Crafternoon. Since it was a valentine-making party, I thought I'd be something of a clever girl by using hearts in the design. I cut lots of little hearts out of construction paper and punched holes in them. On each heart I wrote a letter, and then I strung them together on a piece of multicolored yarn, forming a sign that reads, "Welcome Crafty Girls." (My first Crafternoon in New York was girls only.) Since then, I have added on a new string of paper hearts that says, "& Boys." I tape these little strings to my door each and every Crafternoon as a little ritual. Having a hand-crafted welcome sign is a really nice touch. It gets your Crafters excited about the 'noon before they even walk in the door.

SAY IT WITH FLOWERS

Now, it is the season of flowers, but roses are expensive this time of year. I like a simple vase of red or pink tulips to show the love. I've collected lots of cheap but cool vases at garage sales and stoop sales and flea markets all around this country. I'm a big fan of throwing a great bunch of a single variety of flowers into a cool vase. Tulips don't last as well as some other flowers, but the way they open up indoors makes them a knockout for a party. And I happen to love them when they bend. Their sloping lines remind me to go with the flow, and do a downward-facing dog or two while I'm at it.

MORE, MORE, MORE DÉCOR

You've tackled flowers, but you want something more to adorn the space for those you adore. Why not clear one wall of pre-existing art and make it a wall of hearts? Get a bunch of paper and fabric and cut out hearts of various sizes. Stick them to the wall with some tape and, presto, you've got a hearty mural. And at the end of the day, you just gingerly peel off the pieces and use those hearts to make a second round of valentines. Reduce, reuse, recycle, baby! Adhere them to contrasting colored paper, and you've got a simple, pretty valentine that works for any audience.

If you want to take it further with the decorating, you could drape your house in red satin, light some candles, and turn on some smooth jazz. But then you'd be going crazy. If I came over for an afternoon of crafting and was greeted by couches draped in satin, I'd be a little freaked-out. But maybe that's just me. You're getting ready for a funtastic Love in the Crafternoon, so do it up however you'd like.

CRAFTERNOON QUIZ:
WITH CRAFT I CELEBRATE MY LOVE FOR YOU

St. Valentine was all about love. But how did he get the love reputation? Here's a little history lesson couched in a game—call it a choose-your-own-St.-Valentine adventure. One of these stories is the true story of St. Val. Try to guess which one!

1 St. Valentine was a priest. He lived in Rome in the third century, and he helped young lovers by marrying them. That's not too impressive at first glance, but there's more to the story. See, St. Valentine was marrying the young lovers *despite* the emperor's decree banning marriage. There we go—that's the twist. As everyone knows, going against an emperor's decree is a bad idea. And why the decree, you ask? Well, it seems that Emperor Claudius II was dabbling in some amateur sociology and had come to the conclusion that the single guys in his army were better soldiers than those who had wives or babies back home. An army of bachelors, he reasoned, would be totally devoted to his cause. So he just banned marriage. St. Valentine thought this was incredibly unjust, and he disobeyed the emperor. He performed illegal marriages until he was found out, and then let's just say he slept with the fishes.

2 Some folks say that St. Valentine helped Christians escape Roman prisons, where they were treated with great cruelty. There's no romantic love in that story, but helping people escape persecution is a pretty lovable trait.

3 In the third version of the tale, St. Valentine was imprisoned, and while behind bars, he fell in love with the prison guard's daughter. He'd pass notes to her, expressing his love. It's the classic star-crossed-lovers scenario. I mean, what's more star-crossed than a prison guard's daughter falling for the man behind the bars? Valentine was undeterred by the doomed nature of their love and signed his missives "Your Valentine." So if we choose this story as our go-to Valentine account, when we send a note saying, "Please be my Valentine," we're really saying, "Please be my imprisoned, unattainable lover." That might appeal to some folks. It's certainly something to consider.

4 St. Valentine was the patron saint of bakers. He was known throughout the land for his famous chocolate cake, a cake that was rumored to cause pregnancy when eaten. Ladies in the region who could not get pregnant by more traditional means learned of this story and began flocking to Valentine with requests for a piece of it. But Valentine was a cloistered monk and was allowed to receive visitors at the seminary only one day a year. As the tale of the cake spread throughout the land, the annual Valentine visit turned into something of a wild affair. The seminary would be flooded with desperate women, hoping to receive a piece of the chocolate cake and become fertile. As you may have guessed, Valentine's annual day of visitation was February 14.

So, which one is the true Valentine story? Well, actually, the historians can't decide. The first three are all possible true stories of the patron saint of lovers. Oh, and I made up the fourth one, so don't try to find that cake-filled seminary. It exists only in the recesses of my mind. But let's celebrate the man, the myth, the legend that is St. Valentine with some Crafternoon projects that will make anyone swoon.

LOVE PROJECT NUMBER ONE:

HAVE HEART, WILL TRAVEL

In addition to my mom's seasonally decorated wreath, she also has a seasonally decorated ficus tree. The February love theme is rendered with a gathering of tiny cloth hearts. Hung all over the tree in various sizes and shades of red, they look like huge cherries ready to drop at a moment's notice. My mom does less of the seasonal tree decorating now that we're all grown up, but my brother and I always loved the dressed-up living tree.

To make your own stuffed heart ornaments takes little effort, but they'll be greeted with lots of love. They're a great addition to the rearview mirror, the scented ones work hard to make a linen closet smell good, and they can even be used as a crafty amulet. My best friend, Christine, is not a big fan of flying, so prior to one trip, I gave her one of the little stuffed hearts from my mom's Love Tree. She then began carrying "Mr. Heart" with her whenever she had to brave any air travel. Mr. Heart is small—just the right size to squeeze in the palm of your hand as a plane climbs into the atmosphere. Here's how to make a basic stuffed heart for your main "squeeze."

Supplies
At least one foot of fabric, at least one foot of ribbon, heart-shaped cookie cutter, cotton stuffing or fiberfill, thread, needle, pins, scissors, fabric pen or ballpoint

Optional: *Chopstick, dried herbs*

Step One: *Find some fabric that suits your fancy.* Though a red heart is the old standby, there's no reason why you can't use any color or pattern you like. While you're tracking down your fabric, look for some complementary ribbon. You'll need enough of it to make a little loop for your heart to hang from.

Step Two: *Cut and don't run.* To get a simple heart design committed to fabric, the easiest tool I've found is a cookie cutter. Look for a simple heart shape in the size you desire. If you're work-ing with a big piece of fabric, start from the outside edge and cut a rectangle of fabric slightly larger than twice the size of the cookie cutter. Working with a small piece of fabric makes the process way more manageable. Now, fold your fabric in half so that the reverse side faces out, then pin the fold together in the center. This will act as an anchor when you're tracing and cutting. Lay the fabric on a flat surface, and place the cookie cutter on top of it. Hold the cookie cut-ter in place with one hand and, using a fabric pen or a ballpoint, trace the shape with the other. Cut along the outline, giving yourself an extra ½ inch to accommodate for the seam.

Step Three: *Beautify your coronary creation with bling.* No, I'm not talking about pacemakers. If you want to make a bunch of hearts to give out to all your best boyfriends, you can certainly leave them embellishment free. You don't want them sitting around comparing hearts, trying to decipher which one you love the most. After all, even you can't figure that out! But if you're making a special heart, why not make it that much more special with some embroidered embellishments? Separate your fabric, and work on the "fancy" front face of it. You could sew on your initials plus your loved one's initials. That would be pretty darn adorable. Or for the other half of an on-again, off-again relationship, you could sew little patches on the heart, suggesting that although your love has had some tough times, it will survive.

Step Four: *Sew it up, little darling.* While you can certainly use a sewing machine if you have one, I am pretty sure you'll be perfectly happy with the results you get when you take the hand sewn route. Make sure the front sides of the fabric are facing each other when you start to sew—you'll be turning the heart inside out when you're done to hide the seam. Sew your stitches along the heart's edge with a simple stitch. Don't forget to stitch in the loop of ribbon on one side of the fabric, right between the two bumps of the top of the heart. Leave a small opening toward the central valley of the heart with just enough room to push in some stuffing. It shouldn't be very big because you want it to be discreet when you stitch it up from the outside.

Step Five: *The right stuff.* Turn your sewn heart front side out so it looks like a little sack. Now the fancy side of the fabric is facing the world, and you are ready to fill your heart with love. Using cotton balls or fiberfill or down feathers or cat hair, stuff your heart until it's as stuffy as a country club. (Actually, don't use cat hair. If your valentine is allergic, he'll wind up a sneezy, puffy mess. And a sneezy, puffy valentine is a cranky valentine.) If need be, you can use a pencil or a chopstick to gently guide the filler into the heart's tip. And spice things up with herbs! Adding some dried herbs in with your filler will make for a delicately scented heart. Or simply use the herbs as the sole filler. I like to use herbs that I've grown on my windowsill. Even in a small apartment, you can have a little herb garden as long as you have some sunlight. Lavender is a delightful scent, and it's easy to grow. But if you've only got room for a few pots and you prefer to keep your herbs savory, nurture some sage and oregano. Even those savory scents make for a sweet-smelling heart.

Step Six: *A strong finish.* With delicate stiches, sew up your sweet heart. Take your time so you can do your best tiny stitching. Then show it off to all your fellow crafters and daydream about the great impression you're going to make on your heart's desire with your desirable heart.

LOVE PROJECT NUMBER TWO: A BOX FULL OF LETTERS

Do you remember the valentine-giving ritual at your grammar school? I do. Each child made a box for her or his valentines. Like a piggy bank, the box had a slot in the center of the top where all the valentines were dropped in. This was to ensure maximum discretion. There were no obvious piles on one kid's desk proving how outrageously popular one person can be. And on the flip side, the box that stayed empty would never betray the truth of its loneliness until the owner took it home. I have heard that many schools now have an all-or-nothing policy when it comes to valentines—you give a valentine to every single child in your class or you don't get to give any at all. And quite frankly, I think that policy rocks. Why should schools encourage an atmosphere akin to a popularity contest, when the point of the holiday is to share the love?

Nevertheless, the Love-Letter Bank is a useful and fun project to make at your 'noon. I love keeping old letters, whether they are from friends or boyfriends or family, and it's nice to have a special place to stash them for posterity. Rufus's mom, Susan, made him a really cool box for his high school graduation, and it's a unique and beautiful gift. So make a special box with the power of decoupage. It will be a keepsake for your keepsakes.

Supplies
Box, paint, magazines or other paper images, white glue, decoupage medium, scissors, medium-size paintbrushes

Optional: *Chopstick*

Step One: Boxing day. Find the right box for your love archive. A shoebox was fine for grammar school, but it may not last for the long haul. Cigar boxes are just the thing for storing old sentiments. If you're not into your correspondence smelling faintly like an older gentleman, you can buy a simple wooden box at a craft store. And for those of you who are both wildly popular and totally organized, you'll want a file box. Go to your local home-organizing store and get a box that's designed to hold hanging folders so you can organize the expressions of love you receive. You can have a folder for love letters, one for holiday cards, one for birthdays, one for all the congratulatory notes you've received as you've achieved great success time and time again, and one for all the fan mail you get for just being you.

Step Two: *Make it pretty.* While you don't have to actually make the box look pretty, you do want to make it your very own. And if you're planning to give it away, you want to make it someone else's very own. So decide what look you're going for and then gather your decorations. Postcards look cool pasted all around— they give the box the look of an old trunk with labels from exotic places. Or simply select scraps or sheets from the papers collected for the valentine making. With a variety of paper to choose from, you can create any kind of look. Select your favorite paper images from magazines or photographs, and try placing them on the box in different orders. Once you have a sense of what you want to use and where you want to place it, you can get down to gluing. If you want to paint your box, paint it first, let it dry, and then set about gluing on the paper images.

Step Three: *Make it stick.* Using regular white glue, adhere the paper images to the box. Put glue on the box where you plan to lay your image, then stick the image to the gluey spot, carefully smoothing out any bumps with your chopstick. Apply each image in the same fashion. You can add all sorts of different images to the box, and they can overlap. Let the images dry completely on the box.

Step Four: *Seal the deal.* Using your paintbrush, cover your box with a layer of decoupage medium, which is basically a form of white glue. If the box doesn't look stable once one layer of decoupage medium has dried, you can add another layer of it until it looks good. Let it dry completely, and voilà, you have yourself a keepsake container.

LOVE PROJECT NUMBER THREE:
SENTIMENTAL SKIVVIES

There's no such thing as too much underwear. Laundry day can be avoided till the last possible moment if you're working with a serious stash of underwear. And nobody likes laundry day. So what better way to show your love than to give your loved one personalized underoos? With a fabric pen and some clever phrases, you can turn a boring pair of Skivvies into his or her favorite pair.

Supplies
Underwear, fabric pen or puffy paint

Step One: *Locate the unmentionables.* A simple pair of cotton underwear in the appropriate size will be the best foundation for your panty project.

Step Two: *Take pen to paper.* Before you take permanent marker to cloth, brainstorm some possible taglines. You don't want to get halfway through writing "I Love You" on fabric and suddenly realize, "Man, I haven't even said those words *out loud* yet." Seeing "I Love You" written in puffy paint is known to cause euphoria, but you better mean it before you paint it. So get a pad and a pen and start writing out your feelings. If you're at a loss for words, try to think about popular souvenir T-shirts and bumper stickers, and figure out if you can change the phrasing to make it work for your friend. Here are some examples that can easily be made more specific:

Somebody in _____ *Loves Me* (The more specific, the better, i.e., somebody in Greenpoint, The Mission, West Chester, Apartment 3R loves me.)

Kiss Me, I'm _____ (Again, specificity is king when it comes to personalizing, so for me it would read, "Kiss Me, I'm Three-Quarters Irish, Almost a Fourth Scottish, a Sixteenth French, and a Whole Lot of Awesome." I like to keep my shirts and underwear accurate. And humble.)

Ithaca is Gorges, and So Am I (That's all-purpose. Feel free to use that as is.) You don't even have to come up with a clever phrase to make something cute and customized. If you feel like being a big spender, just get seven pairs of underwear and make a set of days-of-the-week underwear. You'll be the ultimate laundry-day hero.

Step Three: *Put it in writing.* Using puffy paint, a fabric pen, or another detergent-safe marker of your choice, put your thoughts down on your permanent underwear record. Test your writing implement on a piece of scrap fabric before you start writing so you can get a feel for the flow. You can use a stencil if you prefer to have a clean look to your letters, but if you'd rather be free-love style, just write it freestyle. It'll take the gift to the next level of personal appeal.

CRAFTERNOON INTERLUDE:
Where Do Broken Hearts Go?
Um, Crafternoon. Duh.

My friend Mark used to date my friend Sarah. Sarah is a devout Crafternooner. She was present at the very first NYC Crafternoon, the girls-only valentine-making extravaganza. And from then on, anytime I threw a Crafternoon, Sarah always showed up. And once Crafternoon became unisex, Mark didn't start showing up until Sarah convinced him it was a good way to spend a few hours. But Mark was a quick convert to Crafternoon, and soon enough he became a regular. Eventually, he started coming even when Sarah couldn't attend.

But then two years after the founding of the CrafterNation, Mark and Sarah broke up right before Valentine's Day. So when it came time for the Fourth Annual Valentine-Making Crafternoon, I received two somber responses to my email invitations. Both Mark and Sarah wanted to know if the other was going to be at Crafternoon. Each of them really wanted to attend, but neither was ready to face the other. The awkwardness was upon us, and I pondered what to do.

I wanted them both there, but I understood that the Valentine theme would make it an unbearable postbreakup Crafternoon. In my gut, I felt that Sarah would always be a devout Crafternooner, but turning Mark away might sour him on Crafternoon forever. I hemmed and I hawed. And then I realized: You know what, I don't have to decide which one comes to the 'noon! I tactfully suggested that they resolve it among themselves, since I felt that I simply wasn't sage enough to figure it out. And then I waited.

On that Crafternoon, I hadn't heard from either of them. I feared that they had both simply chosen to stay home and craft on their own. But then halfway through the fun, Mark showed up for the crafting and camaraderie. It turns out that Sarah had graciously given up the Crafternoon so that Mark could go. And that is the sign of a love that can make its way into a friendship. And that is also the sign of some strong love of Crafternoon.

LOVE PROJECT NUMBER FOUR:
COLLAGE BOUND! VINTAGE VALENTINES

I love old magazines something awful. Someday I hope to have some flat files of my very own, and when I do, those flat files are going to be filled with old magazines. There's something about old advertisements and photographs that fill me with a sense of comfort. Maybe it's just the handpainted quality of the early color photos or the wide-eyed innocence that seems to seep through every image. Whatever it is, old magazines are an oft-overlooked and highly minable source of great images. I've found that there is nary an occasion that can't be tackled by the right image from an old magazine. Hang on—I'll take that back. I've never felt comfortable making a condolence card. But hey, we're talking valentines! Man, who brought the wet blanket?

Now, I love American magazines from the late 1940s and early 1950s. (I've only ever gotten my hands on American magazines, but I imagine the magazines of many nations from that era have delightful images, too.) Old magazines can be found at flea markets, yard sales, in antique stores, in grandparents' attics, on the Internet—all over the place, really. I used to cut these up willy-nilly, but recently someone suggested that I might be better off making color photocopies and then cutting those up. Geez, some people are so practical. I guess that it wouldn't be a bad idea. If you keep the original magazines intact, you have a renewable resource of images. And then you can avoid the common conundrum that accompanies most magazine cutting: "If I choose the image on this side, I can't use the image on the other side. If I want the image of the family gathered happily around a shish kabob machine, I cannot use the recipe for 'Tall Teen Wiener.'" (Thank you, West Bend Kabob'n Grill, for your priceless recipe and instruction manual. I wish that you still sold these vertical grills with eight roto-matic skewers. I would kabob it up each and every night, I promise you.)

For those of you who don't feel like traveling to your local copy center or sneaking color copies at work, I say, just cut those mags up! Honestly, I think the copying idea is a great one, and that's why I shared it, but I really doubt I am ever going to make that organized dream a reality. When I want to make a card, I want to make one immediately. That's just how I roll.

Supplies
Construction paper, magazines, glue sticks, scissors

Step One: *Work on your image.* Everyone has his or her own reasons for choosing a picture. Me, I love the funny images, and old magazines offer them en masse. You'll find your fill of young lovers innocently holding hands, but you'll also stumble across hilarious food product double entendres and advertisements for all sorts of discreet hygiene products. So whether you're looking for lovers or powders that freshen up, you can find something that expresses how you feel. Just choose a picture that strikes a chord in you.

Step Two: *Cut it out.* Um, yeah. Cut your favorite images out of the magazines. Take your time—you don't want to miscut and screw up your fantastic image. Use a good pair of scissors and a large helping of patience, and you'll cut everything perfectly.

Step Three: *Location, location, location.* Before I commit an image to the page, I like to move it all around and figure out where I might want it to live. Magazine paper tends to be thin and easy to tear, so gluing it and then moving it is not an option. Practice your placement and then make it stick like glue with, well, glue.

Even if it is a Hallmark holiday, you shouldn't be ashamed to celebrate. There's nothing wrong with love, to steal a line from Built to Spill. In fact, love is the best thing in the whole world. So why begrudge the best thing in the whole world getting a day of celebration? Gather your friends, work on your crafts, and get your love on.

CHAPTER THREE

MARCH

CHARITABLE CRAFTERNOON

You know the old adage, "Charity begins at home"? It's a pretty solid adage, and one that inspired me to spend a few years of my life working in the nonprofit world. I used to work with seniors, coordinating volunteers and programs at a time bank. A what bank? That's right, you heard me. Not a food bank, not a money bank—I used to spend my days working at a *time* bank. Time banking is a system of volunteering that encourages people to give back to their own community by providing a service to another person. When you provide the service, you earn a credit, which goes in your time bank. Then when you want to receive a service from someone else, you contact the bank and they find another volunteer who can provide you with that service. And how do you pay for this?

With the time you already earned that is sitting in the time bank! Yeah, it's pretty awesome. Your mind should be blown.

In this sweet time-bank cycle of giving, the line between volunteer and recipient is constantly shifting. No single person is valued over another for his or her ability to give. The program was built on the concept that everyone has something he or she can give, and everyone has something that he or she would like to receive.

One gentleman in our program knew exactly what he wanted to do with his time dollars. Beno, who was a home-repair volunteer, helped his fellow senior citizens all over Brooklyn with their leaky faucets and their wobbly tables and their broken lightbulbs. He heard that some of our other volunteers were homebound folks who would knit or crochet blankets for nursing-home residents and also did sweater repair. He went to my friend Marie, one of the volunteer coordinators, and explained that he had a sweater that needed to be repaired. But this was not just any sweater— this was the first sweater his wife had ever knit for him nearly 50 years ago. He wore the sweater all the time, but his wife, who had repaired it time and again over the years, had recently passed away. Now it was falling apart, and his wife was no longer around to mend it for him. He was visibly shaken by the sweater's disrepair. But Marie promised him she would get it fixed. A knitting volunteer took his sweater and mended it so completely that it looked brand-new. And when he got his sweater back in this fully restored state, he was so ecstatic that he wept. And it was this story of Beno and the ladies who repaired his sweater that inspired me to apply for a job at the company. I hadn't heard of such a wonderful demonstration of community in a long time.

The volunteers who knit and crocheted were a group fiercely committed to their task. They would call us as soon as they ran out of yarn, asking, nay, *demanding* that we send them more. They would bring their beautiful finished blankets to group events, pulling them out of big plastic bags to show them off to one another. And if there was extra yarn, they would throw in the odd craft item—a knit pocket to sling over an armchair to hold your remote and TV guide, a pot holder, a knit cap, or a pair of delicate baby booties. Nothing was left to waste. And each item was infused with an aura of kindness, compassion, and creativity.

Cut to the year 2007. My friend Sabrina was working on a knitting project as an installation piece at a museum. Her piece explored the tradition of knitting during wartime, and as a part of the project, she invited museum visitors to sit in the museum and knit squares to be included in blankets being made for Afghan refugees and wounded American soldiers returning from Iraq. As I began planning for my March Crafternoon, I thought of that project, and I thought of the homebound volunteers crocheting their blankets for nursing-home residents, and I realized that a Charitable Crafternoon was just what the doctor ordered. What could be more rewarding than an afternoon spent creating with friends while giving back to the greater community? Not a whole heck of a lot.

So I invited my Crafternoon crew to knit squares for a blanket to be donated. I found a charity online called Project Linus, which provides homemade blankets to children in hospitals and shelters. I wanted to keep the project inclusive, so I offered to teach anyone who was interested how to knit. And as it turned out, of the eight crafters who attended, three had no prior knitting experience, but those knitting virgins were all interested in learning. So my mom and I laid our squares aside while we showed the three newbies how to begin their adventures in knitting.

It's fun to show someone how to knit, and there are tips on how to do that in the knitting chapter. (Feel free to skip ahead to the November Crafternoon chapter on page 171—I'll be waiting for you when you get back.) Besides, it felt good to know that this Crafternoon was creating good things—squares for a nice blanket and the skills to knit those squares. And I think the new knitters liked the good vibes—I believe it's easier to learn something when you're doing it for a good cause. It was so nice to just sit and knit in a group, and the time flew by. And while we didn't complete enough squares to finish a baby blanket, we made new knitters. My mom and I worked on finishing up the blanket after the 'noon was over. I knit a couple of extra squares, and she knit a few more, and before I knew it she was stitching up the squares and turning the parts into a beautiful, whole blanket to brighten a needy kid's day.

So, get ready to host your very own Charitable Crafternoon! Yeah, I know you're psyched, but how do you get started? There is one simple question to ask yourself when you're starting to make your Crafternoon plans that will help you find your way: Do I want to choose a project that will have a global reach or a local reach?

THINK GLOBALLY, DONATE GLOBALLY

If, like me, you want to do some charitable knitting, there are a few ways to knit for a good global cause. A couple of organizations come to mind right away when I think of global charitable knitting. Sabrina donated her knitted projects to two organizations, one of them being Afghans for Afghans. This group collects blankets, hats, and other homemade garments to donate to refugees from Afghanistan. The blankets are distributed through aid groups working in the area, who include them with deliveries of food and medicine. My mother introduced me to the Mother Bear Project (and as my own Mother Bear, I suppose it is quite fitting that she did so). The project collects handknit bears to distribute to children around the world who are affected by HIV/ AIDS. Knitters are encouraged to tag the bear with a note saying where the bear came from.

ACT LOCALLY, DONATE LOCALLY

The world is your oyster, but when it comes to volunteering your time, you want to give the pearl to someone or something in your community. I understand completely. Sometimes we are so gung ho to help folks in the big world out there that we forget that there are good people right nearby who could use some of our love and affection. So go ahead, give it to them in the form of craft!

Sabrina also gave her knit wares to Flags Across the Nation, in addition to Afghans for Afghans. Flags Across the Nation is a patriotic organization that collects blankets for American veterans. If you need some inspiration, call local organizations and ask them what crafty things they could use. Where should you call? Try schools, community centers, hospitals, nursing homes, shelters, churches, Girl Scouts, etc. If you've got a Crafternooner with a kid, look no further than their school fund-raisers for inspiration. If they've got a charity auction, your group could work together on making something to donate. If they don't have an auction, ask the school if they'd want to set up a fund-raising raffle with your donation as the main prize. Or make it a Bake Sale Crafternoon! Open your kitchen to your crafty friends and whip up some batches of tasty treats. I recommend that some folks bring some already baked items that can be decorated by the group—cupcakes, cookies, donuts, brownies, you name it. Then provide a variety of decorating supplies (including disposable gloves for maximum culinary hygiene) and go to town. Let me tell you, decorated sweets sell for a pretty penny on the bake-sale market.

What if you like the bake-sale idea but aren't in the school circuit? It might be a bit difficult to convince a school to take your homemade goods for their bake sale if they don't know you from a hole in the wall. Sorry, but we don't live on the set of *Leave It to Beaver*, and people are a wee bit suspicious these days. So now what can you do with all of these tasty morsels? Have your own bake sale and donate the proceeds to your favorite charity! Decorate your baked goods in the morning, then get your butts into the great outdoors (or at least someone's front yard) and sell your wares! Be sure to alert your neighborhood with crafty and colorful signs telling folks about the bake sale. Include info about the charity you plan to donate to. It'll be good grassroots marketing for them, and it should give a nice boost to your bake-sale customer numbers. Urban dwellers need not despair—find a sweet spot on your sidewalk or a well-trafficked stoop and you, too, can make your own open-air market.

On a lovely spring day, what could be nicer than spending the morning in food-craft mode and spending the afternoon in the cool breeze, hocking your homemade treats? Or choose a great summer day and spend the morning in a cool room painting waves and umbrellas on cupcakes. Why not anoint a crisp autumn day, and sit on a porch watching the leaves turn while you paint brownies with jack-o'-lanterns? Okay, what I'm trying to say is: Winter is the only time you can't guarantee foot traffic at your outdoor bake sale. But wait a second—if you live in California or somewhere equally warm and pleasant, I suppose you've got delightful weather year-round. If that's the case, then go ahead, make the rest of us jealous and have your outdoor winter bake sale! Decorate tropical fruitcakes with snowmen and have a hearty laugh at those of us sitting in front of our radiators dreaming of spring. We won't mind. We'll be sending you our cold but kind wishes from the seasonal tundra.

Choose one of your Crafternooners to be the treasurer of the bake-sale project. At the end of the day, tally the cash, then donate your earnings to the charity of your choice. And you don't have to give to just one! Split your haul between a few favorite charities that need a little love. If the group can't think of any, I'd suggest that you choose a needy local school and use the money to purchase art supplies for their students. The sad fact is that many schools in this great nation lack the resources to purchase items like crayons and colored paper. Why not be their knight in shining craft armor? Talk to the school art teacher and ask what supplies the students need the most. Then buy them for them! It's just that simple. And wouldn't it be nice to know that your crafting allowed others to craft as well? Yeah, you know it would be totally awesome.

"But hold your horses, Maura! The bake-sale idea isn't for me!" No biggie—we don't have to turn on a single oven or stir an ounce of batter to get the crafty charitable good times flowing. Let's think outside the cake-mix box. You could certainly tackle a knitting project like the ones suggested above, and then donate your cozy end product to a local charity. But I'm getting the feeling you don't want to knit. Some folks have knitting-averse hands that have been impacted by arthritis or carpal tunnel syndrome or another hand challenger. Some folks have had one really bad night with knitting, and now every time they see yarn, they feel nauseated. And some folks might be really young children, and very young children have a tough time with knitting needles. Whatever the reason, be it a latent fear of pointy things or a crowd that has a strong distaste for yarn, you just might not want to knit. I will try to convince you otherwise during the knitting chapter, but for now I'll just let you do it your way.

I believe that Crafternoons should be inclusive events, and there are endless projects to choose from when it comes to craft. One of my favorite group projects can easily be donated toward a charitable end. What is that, you might ask? Make and donate homemade decorations! Um, what, you might wonder? Hear me out on this one. This is how it's going to go down. . . .

Flower arrangements and other decorations are often accepted by nursing homes and hospitals. When your surroundings stay the same day to day, it's nice to have something new and cheerful to look at, and knowing that it was made by hand with you in mind makes it extra sweet. But you can't just make some arrangements and arrive at the nursing home next door, arms full of good stuff. Avoid charitable heartache by checking in with your donation spot before you get down to the crafting. You want to make sure they accept donations and find out what sort of things they are really looking for. Call and ask to speak to someone who handles volunteers and community service. Explain that you'd like to donate some handmade decorations. See if they'd like to take you up on the sweet offer. If they can't accept them, they might know of a community center or another site that does. Now that you have some crafty charitable options, it's time to start rounding up your fellow do-gooders.

GET THE WORD OUT AND SET UP YOUR SPACE

You want to make a difference, so the more difference makers you can gather to craft with, the better. Here's the invitation I sent to drum up attendance at my Charitable Crafternoon:

Charity Begins at Crafternoon

This Saturday, crafters will gather to do something heart-warming—to craft something for someone else.

We're going to knit some squares to be sewn together for a blanket to be donated to a very cool charity that gives handmade blankets to needy kids.

I'm going to bring a bunch of washable yarn with me, along with some extra needles. Feel free to bring some extra washable yarn to donate, if you've got some lying around.

If you'd like to join us but don't know how to knit, I'll be happy to give basic lessons!

If you don't feel like knitting, you can bring along materials to work on any crafty project you've got going on. I won't make you donate it, I promise.

Bring a delicious treat to share or maybe a tasty beverage. I'm looking forward to crafting something with you to give away.

xoxo,

Maura

Since the blanket project requires yarn, you're going to need lots of it on hand. Acrylic, cotton, or washable wool are the varietals you can use for this—regular old wool will shrink up and render your masterpiece a miniature. Now, you could go out and buy loads of yarn, or you could extend the charitable theme by asking knitters to donate some of their own. Most knitters whom I know have some extra yarn on hand, either left over from a completed project or from a time when they overbought in a fit of yarn fever.

You know, like the time you walked into that craft superstore and saw they were having a major sale on neon orange yarn. And you thought to yourself, "With orange yarn selling at such bargain-basement prices, I'm going to knit myself the best full-body Creamsicle costume that Halloween has ever seen!" So you bought pounds of the stuff, and you dragged it home. And there you sat like a mad scientist, drawing up your crazy Creamsicle-costume plans. And then you knit furiously for one unbelievable evening, while visions of you dressed as a giant Creamsicle danced through your head. And then you woke up the next morning, surrounded by balls of yarn and needles, and you gave up. So that yarn is sitting in an orange glowing mass in the corner of your closet.

I'm part hoarder, so it's quite difficult for me to get rid of things without a really good reason. Luckily, donating yarn for a craft project that will, in turn, be donated is definitely a good reason. So open your mouth and ask for some donations. If you are doing a bake sale, ask for baked goods or cake mixes. Whatever you're making, ask your crafters to donate some supplies. And if there is anything left over, you can find nursing homes or homeless shelters or other charities that accept donations. That way, someone else can put it to good use.

TREAT OF THE 'NOON:
Breakfast Burritos for the Hungry, Helpful Masses

After living in San Francisco for five years, I got used to having easy access to cheap and delicious Mexican food. Sadly, in my New York experience, I have yet to find a Mexican place that can compare to my favorite SF haunts. So I've taken the matter into my own hands and started making my own breakfast burritos. Rufus taught me some tricks with beans and guacamole, and I think our homemade treats are pretty damn tasty. I like to go vegetarian for these recipes, but you could certainly add some crispy crumbled bacon or some sausage slivers for a saltier, meatier version.

THE BEANS

½ tablespoon olive oil

1 large onion, white or red, minced

2 cloves garlic, minced

Two 15-ounce cans black or pinto beans

THE EGGS

12 eggs

½ cup milk

Salt and pepper to taste

¼ cup grated cheese (optional)

2 tablespoons butter

THE GUACAMOLE

3 ripe avocados

4 cloves garlic, pressed or minced

1 lime (optional)

THE FIXINS

10 parsnips (optional)

¼ cup olive oil

16 flour tortillas

4 limes (optional)

3 ripe tomatoes

½ cup cilantro

½ cup nutritional yeast (optional)

Beans: Heat the olive oil in a pan over medium heat. When the oil is hot, add the onions. Sauté, stirring occasionally, until just translucent. Add the garlic, and sauté for another 1–2 minutes. Drain the cans of beans, then rinse the beans two or three times. Add the beans to the pan, turning the heat down slightly. As the beans cook, squish them with the back of a wooden spoon to create a thick consistency. Cook 15–45 minutes, until the beans have reached the desired consistency.

Eggs: Heat the oven to 250°F. In a medium bowl, whisk the eggs, milk, salt and pepper, and cheese together until scrambled. In an oven-safe pan, melt the butter over medium heat on the stovetop. When melted, add the egg mixture. Cook over medium heat, stirring occasionally until cooked through. Serve immediately, or cover the pan with an oven-safe lid and store in oven for up to 30 minutes.

Rufus's Simple Guacamole: Peel and pit the avocados, combining the tasty green flesh in a medium bowl. Smash and mix with a fork until combined. Add the garlic, and blend along with the juice of one lime. Mix with a fork until well blended.

The Fixins: Cut the parsnips into quarters, and toss them in olive oil in a roasting pan. Cook them in a 400°F oven for 35 minutes or until browned. Warm the flour tortillas on your stovetop over low heat, heating them 15–30 seconds on each side. No frying pan is necessary, unless you are afraid of an open flame. The flame-phobic can throw each into a dry frying pan for a moment to heat them up. After heating, they will stay warmer if you cover them with a clean cloth napkin or dish towel. Cut the limes into quarters. Chop the tomatoes and the cilantro. Pour nutritional yeast into a bowl for a topping. Serve everything salad-bar style with plenty of serving utensils so your guests can choose how much of each ingredient they want.

CHARITABLE PROJECT NUMBER ONE:
GROUP HUG BLANKET

Supplies
Yarn, knitting needles, yarn needle

Step One: *Decision making.*
Choose your project and review the guidelines for the chosen organization's knit blankets. While the Flags Across the Nation and Project Linus guidelines are quite loose, the guidelines for Afghans for Afghans are more restrictive (wool only, no light-colored blankets, no blankets with images sewn into them, etc.). Choose the right needles for the weight of your yarn.

Step Two: *Cast on!* Cast on 25–40 stitches. *(You decide how many stitches, but keep it uniform within your knitting group. Fewer stitches = smaller squares = better for a baby blanket. Bigger stitches = bigger squares = better for a big-person blanket.)* See page 176 for instructions on knitting.

Step Three: *Knit!* Knit row 1.

Step Four: *Purl!* Purl row 2.

Step Five: *Keep it going.* Complete 30 rows, alternating knit rows and purl rows. Then cast off. You have completed your first square!

Step Six: *Put it all together.* When you have enough squares to make a blanket, lay a clean sheet down on the floor and arrange your knit squares in the order that you wish to sew them together. You could just sew them together at random, but it's fun to see the colors together and figure out the best arrangement. Take a snapshot of your final design, or draw a quick blueprint for your pattern by drawing some squares on a piece of paper and writing a description of the colors in each block.

Pin the squares together in pairs and then start sewing. Divvy up your pairs amongst your crafters so the sewing goes swiftly. Then sew pairs to other pairs until you've got a blanket. And, hey, take a picture of your project and your crafters for posterity. Finally, pop that bad boy in the mail and send it off to the lucky recipient.

CHARITABLE PROJECT NUMBER TWO:

BOUQUET SERA, SERA

Supplies
Vases or jars, flowers, scissors

Optional: Tissue paper, ribbons

Ask your attendees to bring a small bouquet of flowers to the Crafternoon. Gardeners can draw from the bounty of their gardens, and urban dwellers should remember that farmers' markets often have a lovely selection of petals to choose from. Ask everyone to bring a vase they are willing to donate to the project. If you can't rustle up a vase, a mason jar will work just fine, as will any jar that's been cleaned out and stripped of its labels. Any office worker knows that there is usually a stash of abandoned vases collecting dust in the communal kitchen, so post a note asking coworkers to donate their old vases to your project. Most people who have been lucky enough to receive flowers as a gift have at least one generic vase they are willing to give away. Knowing that the beautiful creations you craft will be brightening up the days of others will make this donation an easy sell, especially since it means one less vase for your colleagues to drag home. If you've got jars that still have sticky label residue clinging to them for dear life, then wrap the outside of the jar with tissue paper and secure it with a ribbon. The arrangement will look even more cheery, and you'll hide the unsightly ghost of glue past.

Step One: *Mix and match.* Take all of your donated flowers and organize them by color in buckets or extra vases you've got on hand. Then invite your charitable florists to create bouquets for each vase. It's easiest to arrange the flowers in your hand first and then move them slightly when they are in the vase. Arranging flowers in a vase can be difficult without florist foam, and I hate florist foam because of its weird, possibly toxic dust. So forget about the foam and just deal with your flowers. For design ideas, look at magazines for inspiration, or just throw things together in a way that makes you happy.

Step Two: *Snip snip here, snip snip there.* When you have your happy bunch of stems, measure them against your vase. The general rule is that your blooms should be about two-thirds higher than the top of your vase. Snip the bottoms of the stems so they are even. Stems should always get at least a ¼ inch taken off the bottoms so they can get a fresh drink of water.

Step Three: *Just add water.* Fill your vase about two-thirds full of water. This will give your flowers plenty to drink but help to keep the water from spilling everywhere in transit. To transport your vases, put them in boxes and fill the spaces between the vases with tissue paper. This will keep them stable for their journey.

CHARITABLE PROJECT NUMBER THREE:

THIS LAND IS YOUR LAND, THIS LAND IS GARLAND

Supplies
Construction paper, scissors, glue

Flowers are lovely, but they're not always cheap. In fact, in a city like New York, which is a bed of concrete on top of an island, they are almost never cheap. So you might want to choose a project that's a bit easier on the wallet. Why not leave a paper trail? Paper never ceases to please when it comes to making decorations.

Did you ever make garlands out of paper when you were in grade school? You know, you take construction paper, fold it over several times, and then cut out various designs—kids holding hands, snowflakes strung together, ducks in a row? To make the garland long enough to stretch across the classroom, each kid contributed to the chain with his or her own design. And you'd sit there and watch your friends as they cut their own designs, and when they inspired you, you followed their lead on patterns and techniques, and then you'd look down and see how your shapes were transformed by their influence. But no two sections of garland were ever alike—just like snowflakes. There's something so simple and lovely about that idea—creating a connection between people through paper. Aw, doesn't that make you feel all warm and fuzzy inside? What I'm trying to say is that we're all unique, but there is so much commonality in our experience, too! So let's join our paper hands and decorate this great big world of ours with bright colors.

Step One: *Get the paper.* Procure large pieces of construction paper.

Step Two: *Pleat it.* Fold your paper into evenly spaced pleats, as narrow or as wide as you want them to be.

Step Three: *Draw it out.* On the face of the front pleat, draw or trace the image that you want to replicate. Here are some classics as well as some new options:

- **A person with arms outstretched.** This little guy or lady will form a chain of held hands. This design was first cut in the Paleolithic era by dinosaurs that had large and dexterous hands and a great love of paper decorations.

- **A tulip.** The connector here will be the tulip leaves. You can spice up this decoration by adhering tissue paper to the petal zone after you've made the cut. That will give the tulips some texture and pizzazz. Alternately, you could decorate the petal zone with glitter, sequins, stickers, photos, or anything your heart desires. Live free or die. Am I right, New Hampshire, or am I right?

- **A dachshund.** The nice thing about this design, which takes its cue from the classic Elephants Connected Via Tail Biting, is that the dachshunds will appear to be nibbling on each other's tails. And that, my friend, is *hilarious.*

• **Fans.** And I'm not talking about cutting outlines of people who are obsessed with sports (although I suppose you could do that, if you are feeling the sports fever). No, the fans I'm talking about are the ingenious objects that provide a cool breeze on a hot day and are the perfect thing to peer out from behind when one is trying to be coy with the aristocracy. Cut out a nice line of fans and then decorate them to your heart's content. A string of fans makes for a great summer decoration.

Step Four: *Get it cut and make it stick.* Following your traced guidelines, cut out your shapes. When you're done, glue your garland to the next person's garland, and so on, until you've got a long, lovely paper trail to drape across your recipient's space.

There are so many wonderful projects out there in the world, and these are just some options. Maybe you're thinking to yourself, "Hmmmm, nice ideas, Maura, but those aren't the right projects for me. Why didn't you suggest *my* favorite crafty charity? Or why didn't you think of my awesomely charitable idea?" To which I say, I'm just offering some suggestions! I couldn't possibly list all of the amazing projects and organizations that are out there right now, and I can't predict the kind of cool things that will be created in the future. So how 'bout you do this: Get on the World Wide Web or go to your library and do a search of your own. Don't know where to start your search? If there's a cause that's close to your heart, one that has impacted your life in some way, contact their affiliated society. Ask them if they have a handmade project that you can donate your time and materials toward. And if they don't have one yet, who knows? Maybe your phone call will inspire them to get a craft project going. Heck, maybe YOU can be the one who starts it. Wouldn't that be kind of amazing? Yeah, you know it would. It would be totally amazing!

So, you've had the Crafternoon, you've made your donation, and now what? Well, sit back and bask in the glory of giving. You lucky crafter, you! You'll be giving *after* you've already enjoyed the sweet reward of an awesome Crafternoon. And whether you are donating a handcrafted item directly to a charity or giving them your craftily earned money, talk up your project to everyone you know. Talking is the best way to roll the ball of inspiration along. If you tell someone about your Charitable Crafternoon, they just might be inspired to throw one of their own. And then there will be more giving in the air and more good times. And what the world needs now is more giving and more good times.

CHAPTER FOUR

APRIL

PAPERWORK! (A.K.A. QUILLING WITH MY HOMIES AND PAPERMAKING)

I n America, April means one thing: taxes. Sure, the forward thinking amongst us may have already tackled this ickiest of civil duties, but the rest of us are wrestling with our taxes up until the dreaded April 15. So what better way to excise your paperwork-related aggression than a Crafternoon that explores some crafts that cut, curl, and shred paper to pieces? But I'm not encouraging shady behavior that will land you in white-collar prison. On the contrary, this Crafternoon is a safe space to rip some things to pieces that *aren't* important documents.

This Crafternoon we tackle quilling, a strange and mysterious craft where you roll thin strips of paper into balls and adhere them to bigger sheets of paper to create pointillistic designs. Your friends will be confused when you first mention it—it's so exotic sounding, they've never heard of it! It's some hot paper-on-paper action, and the necessary materials are so simple and ubiquitous that you can probably find them stashed around your pad.

I searched around the Internet looking for the history of quilling, and here's the scoop: Nuns started it. That's right, blame it on the nuns. They would cut off the gilded edges of Bible pages and use the strips to decorate other pieces of text. They were mining the spare environment around them for any materials they could find to get crafty, and even the edges of pages were in play. As a modern-day American, I am lucky to have access to so much of everything. But much like the unspoken rules for an all-you-can-eat buffet, just because you *can* eat everything, doesn't mean that you should. I'm looking at you, America! It's a good rule to keep in mind, in life as in Crafternoon. So each time you set out to prepare for your next Crafternoon, try mining your own space for materials. I bet you'll be pleasantly surprised with what you come up with, and you'll spare your wallet—and some trees—in the process.

GET THE WORD OUT AND SET UP YOUR SPACE

To get my crafters in the mood, I sent the following missive out during a rainy spell in NYC. (It appears that I have something against trees, but that is not true.)

> *Since the trees must be so damn happy with all the rain, we deserve a little something from this equation! Therefore, we, Christine and Maura, and our beloved crafters will devote*

our energies and greatest attention to the craft of paper-related crafts. That'll show those trees!

Craft Project Numero Uno: Quilling

I didn't know what it was until I saw this on the Web. Now I am inspired, horrified, and intrigued. We will have a resident quiller on hand to guide us through the trials of first-time quilling. Confused? Google it!

Craft Project Numero Dos: Paper Dolls with Quilled Garments
Take your newfound quilling skills to the next level by making some sweet outfits for your paper doll doppelgänger.

Craft Project Numero Tres: Papermaking

This is a craft I knew about.. Dumping paper pulp into a vat with water and flowers, only to return with handmade paper! Exciting, indeed. Our resident quilling expert will double as the resident papermaking expert, assisted by those lovelies who have a little papermaking experience under their belts.

As always, you are encouraged to bring your own craft projects and questions. We will try our best to find answers. If you'd like to bring some eats, they are always welcome (and always delicious)! If you'd like to bring crafting materials to share, we think that's grand! And if you'd like to bring other crafty boys and girls along, we'd love that, too!

Get ready to craft,

Maura

Now I want you to gather your supplies and get organized. Here's what you'll need to have a Crafternoon that convinces you that paperwork is fun:

Paper: I know you've got some paper hanging around from previous Crafternoons, so bring that out. If you used it all up, just buy some more colorful construction paper. Or you can recycle your magazines and newspapers for this project. However, if you do this, the paper quality will be lighter, so it might be a little bit more difficult to work with.

Glue: Come on, now—no respectable crafter lives in a house without glue! And even those of us who aren't that respectable usually have glue lying around in case of emergency. So grab your favorite squeeze bottle and get to work opening it. That'll take a while. Man, the person who invents a solution to the sticky glue top should win a prize. Maybe not the Nobel Prize but at least the Crafternoon Award for Excellence. Yeah, I'd happily give that out.

Toothpicks/nails/quills: As a host/hostess with the most/mostess, I can count on you to always have toothpicks. How else do you assemble your famous cocktail kabobs? Pull them out of the back of your utensil drawer and make them earn their keep! If you're more of a carpenter and less of a lady, you could use a nail as your twister tool. If you find one with a wide nail head, that will serve to help stop the rolled paper from sliding off. I also find that a longer nail makes the rolling easier. And finally, there's the porcupine quill. If you've got one lying around, break it out. That's where the term "quillwork" comes from—so show the quill some respect.

Tweezers: It's the social side of you that keeps tweezers at the ready for any plucking needs. So grab your metal pinchers out of your toiletry bag and let's get down to some old-fashioned quilling!

Additional supplies for papermaking: You'll also need to gather up some scrap paper, water, a blender, a screen, and a basin or tub that's big enough to accommodate your screen. You may also want to use pressed flowers, shiny paper, glitter, or dye.

Now that you've got your supplies figured out, let's talk about how you're going to keep your strength up while you papermake. I suggest my great-great-aunt's brownies.

TREAT OF THE 'NOON:
Great-Great-Aunt Mary's Great-Great Brownies

This brownie recipe was handed down by my great-great
aunt Mary. She is doubly great in my ancestry, and they are
doubly great in deliciousness. The recipe is very similar to the
one for brownies found on the box of the unsweetened chocolate squares, so either they borrowed her recipe and threw it
on the box or she borrowed their recipe and claimed it for
her own. I'd like to think they had a taste of her brownies
and decided to immortalize them forever in recipe form on
the package. Either way, they're some classic tasty brownies.

2 squares unsweetened chocolate
1 stick butter or margarine, room temperature
1 cup sugar
2 eggs
2 teaspoons vanilla
½ cup flour
Chopped walnuts (optional)

Preheat the oven to 325°F. Grease a square pan and line it
with waxed paper. Grease the waxed paper.

On the stovetop, melt the chocolate squares in a small pot
over a diffuser. Don't be tempted to taste-test this chocolate—
it doesn't have any sugar in it so it's very, very bitter. In a large
bowl, cream the butter or margarine with the sugar. One at a
time, add the eggs, then the vanilla. Mix in the melted chocolate, then the flour, and finally the nuts. Pour the batter into
the pan and bake for 20–25 minutes, until the brownies have
set. Let the baked goodies cool in the pan for 10 minutes and
then turn out on brown paper to absorb excess butteriness.
Cut while hot. Eat.

I'VE GOT THE SKILLS TO ROLL THE QUILLS

I like quilling because the technique allows me to create an image with depth and texture. And as a person who lacks great skill as a draftsman, I am always looking for new ways to generate images. Quilling is delicate and requires patience, but it's worth the effort. The images that can be created through quilling have a refreshing three-dimensional quality that I haven't found in any other paper craft.

When you're quilling, you're creating a composite picture using rolled strips of paper. It's like a dried bean portrait, except your beans are rolled strips of paper. The paper can be cut as thin or as wide as you'd like to work with. I have a casual approach to crafting, so I don't worry about drawing lines on my paper with a ruler and cutting my strips nice and straight. I just follow the line of the paper and cut my strips freehand. If I did care about straight lines, I'd recommend getting hold of a paper cutter and hacking away. For folks who are überprecise or just lazy, there are stores and craft-supply websites that sell precut strips in all sorts of colors and widths. There are also special tools available for purchase if you become quilling obsessed. The slotted quilling tool is the most practical of them all—you feed the end of your strip of paper into a slot on a cylinder and the slot grasps the paper for you while you twirl it around the cylinder. You can also buy crimping tools that make your paper look like it was braided wet and left to dry in 1985. They've even got crazy-looking tweezers that have a tiny magnifying glass on the end so you can see your mini paper twirls. I don't think I'll ever feel the need to magnify my quilling, but it would be kind of awesome to have some tweezers with a tiny magnifying glass attached.

QUILLING: A QUICK HOW-TO GUIDE

Step One: *Cut ups.* Cut paper into strips ⅛-inch wide. You'll need to cut at least five strips to create any sort of image, and you'll need more strips the more complex your picture becomes.

Step Two: *Rolling, rolling, rolling.* Take one end of a paper strip and pinch it on the end of your toothpick/nail/quill. Going forward, let's refer to the toothpick/nail/quill as your quilling stick. So, using your free hand, wrap the strip of paper tightly around the tip of the quilling stick until there is no paper left to wrap. You want to wrap the paper onto itself, making a coil. You don't want to create a spiral. Carefully slide the coil off of the end of the quilling stick. If you've wrapped it tightly, it will keep its basic shape even after you take it off the stick.

Step Three: *Seal the deal.* Depending on the design you are making, you can either let the coil expand outward to become a larger circle, or you can keep it tightly wound. When you have settled on your coil size, dot the loose end of your paper coil with some glue and press it closed.

Step Four: *Shape it up!* If you want your piece to have more texture, you can create different shapes. Make a loose coil so that you have a flexible form to work with. For a teardrop shape, simply squeeze the coil at one end until it comes to a point, like a tear. For the design that quillers refer to as the marquise, gently anchor the coil at the center with your thumb and forefinger and then squeeze both sides to a point with either your fingers or tweezers, changing the shape to something more akin

to a pointy oval. Don't worry about the quilled piece losing its shape—it won't. When you adhere it to your background with the adhesive product called glue, the shape will be preserved for all posterity.

PAPER PROJECT NUMBER ONE:
QUILL MY NAME, QUILL MY NAME

A simple project to start with is a quilled name plaque that can be displayed in a shadow-box frame. This makes a lovely gift for anyone who has a name. If you feel as though simply quilling someone's name is slightly oddball, you can make it more interesting by quilling "Maura's Kitchen" or "Rufus's Studio" or "Larry's Auto Body Shop." That way the recipient will know exactly where to display the piece. No confusion there.

Step One: *Cut to the chase.* I'd recommend using strips of the same length and width throughout your piece. It will give it a more professional look. Unless you don't enjoy a professional look—then you should simply cut as the mood suits you and see what happens.

Step Two: *Map it out.* For a controlled image, you can draw or mark the outline of the letters on your background paper before you start quilling. That way, when you have the paper balls rolled and ready to go, you can just place them on the line and get the exact design you desire. You can either lightly mark the paper with a pencil or use a chopstick to gently indent the paper where you want your letters to go. If you are using a very light background, the pencil markings may show up. Using the indentation technique can help you avoid that, though it does mean dragging wood along paper, which gives me chills. Me, I like to eyeball my design, so I just skip step two and vibe it out instead.

Step Three: *Stick it!* Following your pattern or your mind's eye, adhere your quilled spirals to your page with multipurpose glue. If you want your design to have flourishes, make teardrops and marquises or even expanded spirals to use at the end points of your letters, especially the capitals. For example, with the letter M, the bottom ends could curve out and end in a big marquise.

Quilling is a craft that can be done piecemeal, and it's a soothing side project. While I was writing this chapter, I was working on a quilled birthday card for my friend Lecy. I quilled her initials in orange paper on the front of a turquoise card. Whenever I was searching for a word or polishing a sentence, I would stop typing for a moment and roll a strip of paper into a quilling ball. It was something active to do with my hands while my brain was on the hunt for information or inspiration. When I finished rolling a ball, I'd decide what size to make it, then seal it with glue and leave it to dry beside my computer, clutched in the metal embrace of my tweezers. It's quite satisfying to craft while you write. Even if you've got a major case of writer's block, if you're quilling while you work, at least you'll have something crafty to show for your time.

CRAFTERNOON INTERLUDE:
Speak to People Who Are Older Than You!

People who are older than you have so many amazing stories, and they want to share those stories with someone. Be the person who listens—you will be so happy you did. I was lucky enough to have my two grandmothers in my life for a long time, and I had the pleasure of hearing many fascinating stories from them. But I have also made many other older friends over the years: grandparents of good friends, family friends, and clients whom I worked with when I coordinated senior-citizen volunteers. I love my elders, and I make it a habit to speak less and listen more when I'm around them. As someone who loves to talk more than almost anything else, this proves to be quite challenging, but it always ends up to be incredibly rewarding. So invite your elders to your Crafternoons, and go sit by them and strike up a conversation. I guarantee you won't be disappointed.

My fiancé, Rufus, has a wonderful family. And in one corner of that family is a lovely little lady named M'Lou. M'Lou is the mother of Rufus's aunt Amanda's husband, Alec. Confused? Don't worry, all you need to know about M'Lou is that she is one fantastic lady. M'Lou is in her 90s, but she's totally hip and up-to-date on all the latest trends in fashion and art (a few years ago, she showed up on Christmas Day wearing black leather pants and a big Peruvian alpaca-wool sweater). But aside from being an enviably fashionable lady, she's also a sweetheart and tells the best stories, as people in their 90s usually do.

So, I'm talking to M'Lou one day and she starts to tell me about her old paper dolls. She says that stashed away in a cigar box, protected from the destructive rays of the sun and the prying hands of grandchildren, lies a pile of paper dolls that she made when she was a child. She had drawn, colored, and cut each one herself, and they had all sorts of costumes that went along with them. Her mother had saved them for her, and she had held on to them. I couldn't believe it. I demanded to view them as soon as humanly possible. I had to see these little paper treasures with my very own eyes.

A few months later, M'Lou brought her cigar box over to Amanda's house and laid out the dolls on the dining room table. They were phenomenal. Each doll was delicately designed and cut, and the characters ranged from tiny cherub-faced baby paper dolls with baby clothes to slinky ladies with bobbed hair and a profusion of glamorous dresses. I'm a total sucker for clothes, and there on the dining room table were tiny paper fashion fantasies, the designs of an incredibly talented teenager from the 1920s. The paper dolls are fashion time capsules. But more than that, they are the manifestation of hours of happy crafting that took place 80 years ago. I told M'Lou that these dolls should be displayed for all to see—she should donate them to a museum, display them in her home, or frame them for her granddaughter's room. M'Lou was flattered as all get out, but she laughed off the idea.

Several more months later, I found a copy of *Folk Art* magazine in my mailbox. Put out by the American Folk Art Museum in New York, which is one of the *best* museums ever, the magazine features a few major crafting trends each quarter. I opened my copy and there, displayed across page after glossy page, were images of old handmade paper dolls! Man, I love it when I'm right.

Seeing M'Lou's dolls and reading the article made me think that making paper dolls would be a great project for a Crafternoon. Although I didn't play with paper dolls as a kid, I did enjoy drawing fashion plates. But paper dolls are just a way to give your fashion plates life and a backstory. M'Lou's dolls had names and personalities: My favorite by far was the glamorous movie star named Angela Hollywood. How great is that? And the dolls' owner has the ability to change the dolls' clothes as often as he or she wants, as long as he or she has a sheet of paper and some pencils. I really like that sort of creative possibility. It's a fashionista's dream come true. So here are the basic steps to making your very own paper doll with—you guessed it—quilled outfits.

PAPER PROJECT NUMBER TWO:

PAPER DOLLS WITH QUILLED GARMENTS

Supplies
Posterboard, colored pens or pencils, scissors or X-Acto blade (X-Actos are X-rated: For adults only!)

Optional: *Paper doll stencil*

Step One: *Draw it out.* To make a paper doll, start with some white posterboard. My mom is not a huge proponent of paper dolls—she thinks they are too fragile to play with. So I figure that making the doll on thicker stock takes care of that problem. Besides, paper dolls are rarely the targets of much thrashing. (Unless they are Led Zeppelin paper dolls. If you are making Led Zeppelin paper dolls, you are making dolls that are begging to be thrashed.) Draw your doll freehand, or purchase a paper doll stencil and trace the outline. Then, using colored pens or pencils, draw the basic details on your doll. Traditionally, the doll sports either a close-fitting outfit or some modest undergarments underneath whatever you dress her in. But hey, it's your doll. If you want the base outfit to be a spacesuit, go for it. Nobody looks bad in a spacesuit, right?

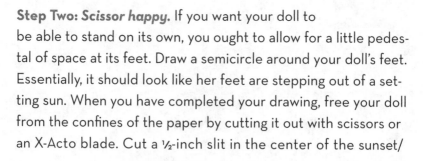

Step Two: *Scissor happy.* If you want your doll to be able to stand on its own, you ought to allow for a little pedestal of space at its feet. Draw a semicircle around your doll's feet. Essentially, it should look like her feet are stepping out of a setting sun. When you have completed your drawing, free your doll from the confines of the paper by cutting it out with scissors or an X-Acto blade. Cut a ½-inch slit in the center of the sunset/

pedestal, then perpendicularly insert a slice of thicker paper a ½-inch high into the bottom of the pedestal, creating a cross section. This will give your dolly a leg to stand on.

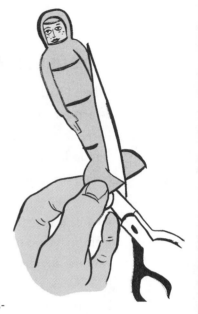

But where does the quilling come in, you ask? (I know you're really feeling this quilling stuff by now. It makes everything more textured and more tactile and just generally more inviting.) Well, why not quill some outrageously amazing costumes for your favorite paper dolls? I'm thinking that your Elton John circa 1975 paper doll would be really happy if you replicated his rhinestone-studded Dodgers baseball uniform using shiny metallic paper. And your Joan Crawford paper doll won't be dressed to impress if she hasn't got a quilled fur coat draped across her shoulders. And she can share the wealth by loaning her fur coat to Elton when it gets cold outside. If you're more of a history buff, then make your own Austrian-born French queen! Your little Marie Antoinette will look exceedingly regal if you make her a trousseau filled with quilled wigs. And it won't hurt to make her some quilled cakes—she's got to have something to let them eat.

Step Three: *Clothing the doll.* Trace the shape of the doll onto a new sheet of paper and give the doll some new threads! Remember to include shoulder tabs so that the garments have some way of staying on the doll. The quilled garments can be made in the same basic way—just adhere the quilling to the garment when you're done cutting out the basic shape and you've got a quilled-out paper masterpiece.

PAPER PROJECT NUMBER THREE:
DOUBLE DIY—QUILLING ON HANDMADE PAPER

When I had my quilling Crafternoon, we weren't just quilling; the afternoon was more like a celebration of paper. So we decided to make handmade paper. Please note: I said "handmade," not "made from scratch." To make paper from scratch, you'd start by roving the woods with your trusty ax, taking out some trees. And that would just be step one. So rather than sending you out on an anti-arbor mission, I'd suggest you make your handmade paper from recycled materials instead. For recycled papermaking, you can use any extra paper you've got lying around—scrap paper from work, tissue paper from retail purchases, paper towels you bought in bulk. Napkins from take-out deliveries work well because they're thin and white and you never know what to do with them anyway. (Note to thrifty crafters: When the delivery person comes a-knockin', don't use his diner-sized paper napkins and his disposable wooden chopsticks. Save them for craft projects just like this one. I've used plastic spoons as paint mixers, chopsticks to unclog glue bottles, and napkins to make recycled paper. Besides, you don't need to use his paper napkins 'cause you use cloth napkins when you're at home. Right? Man, I hope I'm right. If you don't already have some, skip ahead to the June Crafternoon on page 101 and read the instructions on how to personalize some cloth napkins of your very own. I want you to really rock the earth with your friendliness.) You can also use newspaper, but the paper it makes will have a grayish tint to it. For fans of the color gray, this is wonderful news. For the rest of us, a more neutral color is preferable.

Supplies
Scrap paper, water, a blender, a screen, a basin or tub that's big enough to accommodate your screen

Optional: *Felt or chamois cloth, rolling pin, pressed flowers, shiny paper, glitter, dye*

I should note that papermaking is messy. So if you prefer to keep your Crafternoon small and tidy, this may not be the project for you. It's the craft equivalent of mud wrestling. When I had my papermaking Crafternoon, my friend Lori brought along a four-year-old papermaking expert who described the pleasure of the process in the astute way that only a four-year-old can. Her arms were elbows deep in paper slop, when she said, "Ew! It's disgusting! I don't ever want to take my hands out 'cause it feels so good." A most ingenious paradox, wouldn't you say?

The recipe for papermaking is **one part paper to four parts water.** The basic papermaking process is this:

Step One: *Rip it to shreds.* Tear your big pieces of paper into small pieces of paper and dump them into a blender filled with water. Puree the water–paper mixture.

Step Two: *Water it down.* After the mixture is totally pulverized, fill your tub or basin with water. Add the pulp to the basin, and swirl it around until it's all mixed up.

Step Three: *Screen it!* Dip the screen into the water–paper concoction, and cover it with a layer of pulp. At this point, you could set the screen to dry on a flat surface, but then your screen couldn't be used again until the paper is dry enough to remove it from the screen. If you want to use the screen again immediately, turn the paper out on a piece of felt or a chamois cloth (which is typically used to dry wet cars quickly). Using a rolling pin, roll the excess water out of the paper. The cloth should absorb most of the water, but a few puddles could result on your first try, so you might just want to throw a tarp on the floor to keep everything peachy keen and clean.

Step Four: *You've got options.* If you're adding optional elements like petals or dye, you can do so during the basin stage of the process. (You don't want to toss your petals into the blender un-less you're going for a pureed petal vibe.) If you want a red dye, beet juice is natural and stains the heck out of things. Smashed blueberries make a nice purple dye. Experiment with various fruits and veggies to get cool natural colors. However you choose to play with your paper, you better believe this Crafternoon is gonna be one of pulpy fun!

CHAPTER FIVE

MAY

JEWELRY-MAKING MADNESS

I like junk shops and flea markets and thrift stores and yard sales and any other place that sells secondhand things. I love buying something that's already had a life with some-one else, an experienced thing—something that's been around the block and could tell me stories like you wouldn't believe.

On a recent trip to the lovely state of Maine, Rufus and I happened into a low-budget antique store. The building looked like a big shed, and inside there was a pleasant mix of really old books and medium old toys and very old quilts and lots of old, old wooden furniture. As we walked around the store, I picked up lots of cool things I desired, including some ceramic roosters, pictures of old-fashioned-looking women cradling old-fashioned-looking babies, and a game that was supposed to replicate a computer and looked like a Lite-Brite. But I am trying to reduce apartment clutter, so I ended up buying only a little ivory-colored plastic sailboat that was attached to a fragment of knotted rope. The tag said "$2—window shade pull." I liked it, and it wouldn't take up any space in my apartment, so I bought it.

I wasn't quite sure what I would do with it until a few days later. I was riding the subway to work when I started daydreaming about my little white sailboat. I imagined myself on a life-sized version of it, the cool summer breeze on my face, the deep blue sea glistening beneath me. Just like living inside a Christopher Cross song, I imagined sailing taking me away. And then the boat anchored offshore, and I dove into the azure blue water. I exited the water, a crafty Bo Derek, and the closeup revealed that I was wearing a super-hot sailboat necklace. Yes, my little white sailboat that started this whole crazy dream was hanging from my neck like an amulet. And then my mind snapped back to reality. Holding on to the buttery subway pole, I thought, "Hey, at the top of the sailboat, there's a little loop that the rope slid through. So I could just cut off the rope and feed a ribbon through the loop and make it into a pendant for a necklace."

Later that week, as I revisited my sailboat fantasy, I wondered how long it would take to braid my hair into cornrows. I also thought about the necklace, and I realized, "Hey now, maybe this necklace should be more than just a sailboat on a ribbon—maybe it should be a sailboat hanging from two ribbon braids!" A sailboat hanging from braided ribbons would lend a nostalgically preppy air to any outfit, and it would become the perfect addition to my summer wardrobe.

So that Friday night, I kicked it home style and made my own mini-Crafternoon. Rufus was playing music in the living room with his friend Brendan, so I went into the bedroom for some private crafting. I found my little sailboat stuffed in my purse, then I carefully cut the rope from the loop. I spotted a red-and-white gingham ribbon draped over a chair, in the same spot where it had lain since I had saved it from a box of chocolate. Then I dove arm-first into my ribbon drawer. After fishing around and reintroducing myself to some great ribbons, I found an electric blue satin number. Perfeckkk! The plain matte quality of the red-and-white ribbon looked amazing against the shiny blue ribbon. And my blue ribbon was the same width as the red-and-white gingham one but a couple of yards longer. I cut it to match the length of the red-and-white checked ribbon, then cut it again to make a third matching strand. Voilà! I had three lengths of ribbon, enough to make a red-white-and-blue braided extravaganza.

There is something so nice about just diving into your materials and seeing what you come up with. And there's something really nice about staying home on a Friday night and crafting your heart out. It's much better than staying home on a Friday night and crying your heart out. And actually, if you're going to stay home on a Friday night and cry your heart out, you might as well craft your heart out, too. At least you'll have something special to show for it in the morning. Not that those weird red splotches under your eyes aren't something special! And if you decide to craft yourself to sleep, you might just stop crying. Crafting has a nice way of helping the mind shift focus. Yeah, you can't always get what you want, but Mick Jagger taught us all that you just might find you get what you need. And I think what you need is a shiny new necklace.

GET THE WORD OUT AND SET UP YOUR SPACE

Here's the invitation I sent to myself that crafty evening:

Dear Me,

Hey there, Crafty Girl! Feel like crafting up a spontaneous storm? No need to wait for the crafty crowds—go ahead and have yourself a crafty little evening. You'll make some quality jewels and spend some much-needed quality time with yourself. And won't that be nice for you? Bring some grub, have a glass of vino, and get down to some serious crafting.

Time: *Now*

Place: *Here*

Reason: *There's no time like the Crafty Present*

xoxo,

You

TREAT OF THE 'NOON:
Dainty, Delicious Finger Sandwiches Fit for a Debutante

If you're going to be doing delicate crafting, you want your food to be delicate, too. What food speaks more volumes on delicacy and lady-likeness than the finger sandwich? Usually found in British teahouses and movies from the 1950s, finger sandwiches easily make the transition to a rollicking modern-day Crafternoon. And like all sandwiches, you choose the filling, so you can fill them cheaply or you can fill them with gold. Start with white bread, thinly sliced (fresh from a bakery, if possible), with crusts removed. Then layer any of the following filling combos to make some tasty treats fit for your fingers . . .

The Mayflower Club: Thinly sliced cucumbers and cream cheese.

The New Yorker: Smoked salmon, cream cheese, and watercress

The Frisco Farmers' Market: Daikon radish and honey goat cheese

The Fighting Irish: Roast beef and arugula with mayonnaise and horseradish

SUPPLY TIME

Gather up all of your favorite ribbons, pendants, Sculpey clay, water-based acrylic paint, small paintbrushes, Shrinky Dinks plastic, brooch pins, strong glue, an oven, scissors, an X-Acto blade, and colored pencils. You want to have your supplies out and at the ready.

Now, for a solo crafting experience, most people would order takeout or make themselves a simple meal. But not me—there was no way I was going to treat myself any different than any other guest! No, I pulled out all the stops for myself and made myself a massive spread of finger sandwiches.

The Sushi Chef: Smoked salmon, avocado, and cucumber strips
The 91st Street: Cream cheese and ham
The Sweet Susan T: Fresh lobster salad with mayonnaise and a dab of ketchup

To assemble your sandwiches, simply spread the condiment elements on the bread and then layer your ingredients, topping them with the second bread slice. Don't layer your sandwiches too high—remember, these sandwiches are for dainty eaters, not lumberjacks. Cut the sandwich at a diagonal down the middle, then cut them again down the middle, resulting in little triangles. Stack the triangles on a plate, and refrigerate until about 15 minutes before you are ready to serve them. Be sure to cover them tightly in plastic wrap until serving time since white bread has an incredible ability to dry out quickly.

Okay, the truth is that I didn't make myself all of these sandwiches for my solo craft extravaganza. That would be enough to feed a craft army! But trust me on this—if you ever have a tea party, follow these instructions and it'll be a surefire hit.

JEWELRY-MAKING PROJECT NUMBER ONE:
FOUND NECKLACE

Supplies
Pendant, ribbon, scissors

Optional: *Necklace closure or craft wire*

Step One: *Discovery.* Find an item that demonstrates all the qualities of a good pendant: funny, easy to talk to, smart, kind, and creative. Oh, wait, those are the qualities of a good boyfriend. The qualities of a good pendant are: cool looking, having a hole that a ribbon can fit through, funny, and easy to talk to.

Step Two: *Ribbons and bows.* Find some ribbon that is the right width to fit through the top of your pendant. At least two contrasting ribbon colors will make your braid pop, and three will make it psychedelic. But feel free to use just one type of ribbon for a subtler effect. I hear that subtlety can be effective under certain circumstances, though I've never tried it.

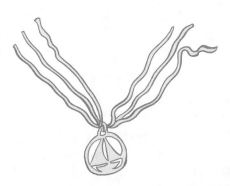

Step Three: *Cut it down to size.* Cut the ribbon into three equal lengths. Then loop the ribbons through the pendant and let the pendant drop to the middle. (There should be equal lengths of ribbon on either side of the pendant.) Tie a simple knot around the pendant to secure it.

Step Four: *Braid it, baby!* Take your time to braid each side of your ribbon chain in the right way. If you get lumps and bumps along the way, go back and rebraid. You want this to look nice, don't you? Or maybe you like the lumps! If you like it lumpy, feel free to braid it lumpy. If you like it flat, braid it and rebraid it until you get it right. When you come toward the end of each braid, knot it closed. Then you can do one of two things:

• **My way:** Leave the knot ends free. When wearing the necklace, tie it closed and have the fringe showing on the back of the neck.

• **The highway:** Cut the fringe off the ends of the knots, and seal each closed with glue. Then attach a necklace closure, available at bead stores and craft stores. Alternately, using thin craft wire, wrap the wire around the sealed ends to create a hook on one side and an eye on the other.

Here's a general jewelry trick that requires no crafting: If you've got a brooch, you can turn it into a pendant by simply dropping it on a chain. I figured out this trick a few years back, and it instantly quadrupled the number of pendants available to me for my accessorizing needs. I also love using old buttons on necklaces. They don't always lie as well as pendants, but if you're lucky enough to find one with two holes, it will lie flat and be a lovely, weird piece to wear around town.

JEWELRY-MAKING PROJECT NUMBER TWO:
HANDMADE OPEN-FACED LOCKETS

Back in the day, ladies wore lockets around their necks. Inside these lockets were pictures of their loved ones—their husbands, their children, their mothers, or their dogs. The lockets kept these loved ones close to their hearts, right where you want your loved ones to be. In our techno-tastic society, we can access images of our loved ones 24 hours a day, using cell phones and computers and digital cameras and so on. But wouldn't it be nice to keep your beloved right nearby, no mouse clicks necessary, just a flip of the clay?

Supplies
Sculpey clay, X-Acto blade, oven, water-based acrylic paint, paintbrushes, cord

Step One: *Molding.* Take your clay and roll it around between your hands until it is malleable. Mold it into a simple shape—the traditional oval or heart shape will work nicely, as will as a square, a rectangle, or any shape you desire. If you know what picture you plan to slip between the clay, try to make the locket big enough to accommodate the image. If you are undecided on the picture, make the locket any size you desire. Just remember, clay is heavy, so a big locket is going to be a heavy locket.

Step Two: *Refining.* Flatten the shape on one or both sides, unless you like the lumpy look. Using a separate piece of clay, add a loophole to the top and mold the loop until it adheres completely to the locket.

Step Three: *Cutting.* Using the X-Acto blade, cut out the center of the clay to create a frame. Use the blade to carefully scrape away the center so that it is relatively flat. The photograph of your beloved will cover up the center, so it doesn't need to be perfect. Alternatively, you could cut off a slice of your locket, place it flat on the table, cut out the center, and reattach the newly created "frame" by molding it to the clay with your fingers. This will give you a flatter center spot. At the top of the locket, cut a slit thick enough to slide a piece of paper through it. If you're concerned that the photo might slip out, create a double loophole, one on either side of the opening. Then when you run the cord through the hole, it will act as a barrier. If desired, cut patterns into the clay using an X-Acto blade.

Step Four: *Baking and painting.* Following the instructions on your clay packaging, bake your clay locket in the oven till it's done. Let it cool, then paint your locket with the color of your choice. If you want your locket to have old-school appeal, paint it gold. Let the paint dry, insert your beloved's picture, and thread it on a cord. And if the picture doesn't stick, dump some glue in the center and *make* it stick. And then rock out with your locket out.

JEWELRY-MAKING PROJECT NUMBER THREE:
SHRINKY DINKS BROOCHES

Who remembers Shrinky Dinks? Raise your hands. For those of you not raising your hands, Shrinky Dinks is the material used for the design and creation of shrunken plastic. Sound intriguing? It is. My mom gave me a Shrinky Dinks brooch a few years ago. She had picked it up at a craft museum store, and I loved it. So I think you should make your own and then we can be twinsies.

Supplies
Shrinky Dinks plastic, colored pencils or pens, oven, brooch pin, strong glue

Step One: *Draw your own conclusions.* The Shrinky Dinks process begins with a paper-thin piece of plastic. Using colored pencils or pens, draw an image on the surface of the plastic in whatever size you like. (You make your drawing on the rough side of the sheet.) Remember, the plastic shrinks when you cook it (hence the name, duh), so read the instructions and make it big.

Step Two: *Cut it out and bake it up.* Cut the image out of the sheet, put it on a baking sheet covered in aluminum foil, and bake it in the oven following the manufacturer's instructions. Keep your windows open when you're baking—this stuff smells slightly funky.

Step Three: *Glue it!* After your shrunken brooch cools off, stick it to your brooch pin and call it a day.

Jewelry adds spice to any outfit, and handmade jewelry makes for a totally unique look. So break out your new baubles and show off what you can do at a Crafternoon for just you!

CHAPTER SIX

JUNE

NOTHING BUT NEEDLEPOINT

I am always looking for new crafts to introduce at Crafternoon, and I often look no further than my own home. One morning I was getting dressed when I stumbled upon my bargello belt. Bargello is a type of needlepoint characterized by geometric patterns, and my belt was crafted by none other than my own mom, back in the Stitchin' Seventies. The belt is stitched with thick wool yarn in red, white, and black, and is backed with a red-, white-, and black-striped ribbon. The belt is almost six inches wide, and it's a killer addition to any wardrobe. Every time I look at this crafty belt, I imagine the good times my mom had when she wore it, and it inspires me to put it on and have a rocking good time myself. That morning, as I examined the bold, simple stitches, I felt a flash of inspiration—bargello would be the perfect project for a Crafternoon!

Now that I'd decided on hosting a bargello-themed Crafternoon, I felt compelled to learn more about the history of this crafty pastime. I had a vague memory of my mother saying that bargello is a stitch invented by prisoner dwellers. I imagined big, tattooed men bent over delicate pieces of canvas, nimbly moving condemned hands to make wild patterns. So I asked my mom to confirm this info. Mom dug out her old copy of *Bargello: Florentine Canvas Work* by Elsa S. Williams for some answers. According to Ms. Williams, the origin of the craft is in dispute. (I always like a little intrigue along with my craft!) Some say that the inmates at the Bargello prison in Florence practiced this craft in the 17th century. Others say it is Hungarian in origin, and the current spelling is a mistranslation of the Hungarian. I like the prison story better. I've said it before and I'll say it again: Crafting is a great way to keep your mind off your circumstances, and prison seems like the kind of circumstance you'd like to keep your mind off. Yes, crafting is a great way to keep your mind off your circumstances. See, I told you I'd say it again.

I told my mom I was interested in trying to rock the barge' at my next Crafternoon, and I asked her if she thought it might be a manageable project. When any Crafternoon project comes to mind, I always consult my mom immediately. I can count on her to tell me if the project can be demonstrated in a single Crafternoon, or if it's just too complicated. The complications usually exist in the form of large or expensive equipment. For example, I would love to do a Crafternoon o' Lathing, but I don't have a lathe, nor do I have access to one (at least not one any closer than West Chester, Pennsylvania, where the father of my friend James, Jim Senior, is a master lathe man). Anyway, since I am lucky enough to have this crafty mom as a ready resource, I always turn to her for her crafty input. But Crafternooners lacking crafty ancestors need not throw their hands up in anguish. There are many resources for answers to craft conundrums. As a matter of fact, this book is a great resource, and I'll point you to others in the very last chapter. Oh, resource foreshadowing! Aren't you intrigued? In any event, my mom felt certain that bargello was a manageable Crafternoon project.

Now, needlepoint is often perceived as a complicated and intimidating craft. But most crafts are as simple or as complicated as you want them to be. As a low-impact crafter, I enjoy simpler types of needlepoint, and bargello needlework focuses on patterns, so it's easy to get into a groove with it. The patterns can range from the very simple to the very complicated, but even the simple patterns are striking in their design. Still not convinced? Well, if you throw in that story of the stitching prisoners, you've got your hands on a legendary craft.

After completing the research phases of planning my Crafternoon, I was on to logistics. I used to host every Crafternoon at my house, but then I moved into a much cheaper (and subsequently smaller) apartment. Since the move, I've started asking other people to offer their space for the event. I still take care of all of the logistics, from sending invitations to bringing supplies to cleaning up at the end, but now other people are more involved. It's actually been a nice change. If you're initiating a regular Crafternoon, you can see if other people are interested in sharing hosting duties on a revolving basis. It makes it even more of a communal effort. And each house you host in will have a different special quality, whether it's great natural light or awesome craft supplies or inspiring art on the walls, which will add a fun, surprise element to your 'noons.

So I checked in with my friend Lori. She is an incredibly crafty lady with an awesome space enlivened by inspiring interior design. We talked out the bargello idea, and she was into it, so we figured out a date and a time for the next Crafternoon.

GET THE WORD OUT AND SET UP YOUR SPACE

My mom helped me create a supply list for our Crafternooners. As you've probably figured out by now, the supply list is important. Here's an abridged version of the invitation I sent out for the Bargello Crafternoon:

Hello, Crafternooners! This Saturday, Crafternoon gets into the sticky summer heat with a hot new craft! My mom will be teaching a little bargello, a foxy type of needlepoint that is wicked design-y. Needlepoint is sure to be the next hot craft trend. Embroidery will also be addressed to show another side of needlework.

For learning the barge', you'll need:

*• **Canvas.** My mom recommends a 10- or 12-count canvas 'cause it's big and easy to work with. You want a piece at least seven inches by three inches. Most craft stores and yarn stores should have it. And of course, if you live near a needlepoint store, they should have some there. If not, check the Internet.*

*• **Ribbon** (two inches thick by six inches long)*

*• **Some yarn.** You'll want to use three-ply yarn for the 10-count canvas and a two-ply for the 12-count canvas. Grab a few colors so you can create some patterns. You also need a*

nice, thick needle. A needle size 18 or 20 should work well. The needle should have a relatively blunt end, making it easier to work with.

• **Graph paper and colored pencil**

For the T-shirt and the napkin embroidery projects, you will need:

• **Embroidery floss** *of various colors, embroidery needles, scissors*

• **T-shirts**

• **Cloth napkins**

• **Optional:** *Embroidery hoop*

As you know, Crafternoon is all-inclusive, so feel free to bring along any craft project you'd like to work on. No need to needle, just come on out and do your craft in good company. Please bring along something to share with your fellow Crafternooners. Sweets are great treats, savories sustain the crafty beast, and beverages are needed to hydrate the thirsty crafter. Feel free to contact me with any craft questions!

Crafternoon forever,

Maura

At the bottom of the email, I also included links to a few bargello-related sites I found on the Internet, including one created by The American Needlepoint Guild that offers a simple description and example of what a basic bargello stitch looks like. I searched bargello and found another site with some great images of old pieces of bargello. I thought the grainy black-and-white photos would give my fellow 'nooners' brains lots of room to run wild with imagined colors. Use Amazon.com to find old copies of some of the best bargello books (like the one by Elsa S. Williams that my mom has).

Sending some links about the craft you'll be tackling will give people a chance to see what it is all about. Using an Internet search engine such as Google, you'll be sure to find great examples of almost any craft. Sure, your friends could do the search for themselves, but you never know what they might come up with. When I looked online, many of the links were focused on quilting with bargello patterns, so I weeded through the results for my buddies so they could go directly to sites that would inspire their Crafternoon desire. If you are mailing your invitations, you can print out and photocopy images of your craft and include it in your mailing.

When the afternoon arrived, I went to my friend Lori's house early to see if she needed a hand with anything. (When I am hosting a Crafternoon at someone else's house, I always arrive before the other guests to help out.) Lori had everything under control, including a beautiful spread of cookies and snacks and several iced teas to choose from. I brought along my grandmother's ever-popular recipe for blondies.

TREAT OF THE 'NOON:
Bargello Blondies (a.k.a. Mrs. Wall's Golden Blondies)

This recipe is for a deliciously sweet treat that will keep your Crafternooners energized with sugary goodness. My grandmother made these brownies for decades, and when my many cousins went off to college, she was famous for shipping these bad boys off in care packages. They hold up well in the mail, probably because they are made almost entirely of sugar. The recipe may not call for sugar outright, but the sweetened condensed milk has plenty of sugar in it. So these blondies have got enough secret sugar and chocolate in 'em to get you through a marathon Crafternoon session. Warning: There won't be any leftovers, so make a double batch if you want some for later.

When the guests started arriving, my mom and I showed them patterns from an old bargello book she had found in her craft arsenal. There were a lot of great examples, both in color and in black and white. Everyone flipped through the book until they settled on a pattern they liked most. Then my mom gave us a few needle pointers to get us started, and we were off!

The pattern I chose to work on was übersimple—a zigzag. I figured a zigzag belt was sure to give me a touch of Charlie Brown charm, minus the dull color scheme. My mom had brought along some yarn for me, and a little turquoise, a little blue, and a little yellow were all I needed to get my belt going. My mom decided to work on a cute little geometric flower.

I like bargello because I can use the patterns as a guideline, but I don't feel encumbered by them. Patterns are really just suggestions anyway. The best way to make a craft piece memorable is to let your personal style shine through the craft. For me, this meant

2 cups graham cracker crumbs
1 stick melted butter
One 14-ounce can sweetened condensed milk
1 cup semisweet chocolate morsels
Dash of salt
1 teaspoon vanilla

Preheat the oven to 350°F. In a bowl, mix all the ingredients together with a wooden spoon. Grease a 11 x 7½-inch pan and line it with waxed paper, then grease again. Bake for 35 minutes. The blondies should be firm and golden when they pop out of the pan. Let them cool for 10 minutes, then turn them out onto a brown paper bag. Cut while hot. Eat till you can't eat any more.

the subtle change of creating a fade pattern, alternating the thread color as I went along, whenever I felt I wanted a change. And that is part of the pleasure of crafting—starting with one idea and watching it transform in the making.

While my fellow Crafternooners and I freestyled, whenever one of us would come to a fork in the craft road, or a knot in our craft rope, we could turn to other crafters for assistance. And, as you may have already guessed, we usually turned to my mom. She has the answer to nearly every craft question known to man. Well, aside from glassblowing and metalwork. I mean, sure, my mom's toured a glass studio and she's probably got a basic understanding of metalwork, but I don't think she's soldered anything on her own watch (at least not yet).

As with every Crafternoon I've thrown, some people came ready to work on alternative crafts, so while some of us worked on bargello, others did their own craft projects. Lori, the hostess, had several projects to work on, and while we needled away, she made a small clay mirror and a few cool hair accessories. Her boyfriend was working on a small puppet of Karl Rove, and another friend was just hanging out. That's the wonderful thing about Crafternoon—you don't even need to be making something to enjoy the good times.

I took some time out of my bargello schedule so that Lori could show me a bunch of the cloche-style hats that she's collected and made. My favorite was an old-fashioned bathing cap she'd made. In this day and age, with my pale paleness, it wouldn't be a bad idea to wear a bathing cap for scalp protection at the beach. I immediately started thinking that a hat Crafternoon should be added to my long list of CrafterNotions, and then I settled back down to my bargello belt. See? There's nothing more inspiring than a Crafternoon.

STITCHERY PROJECT NUMBER ONE:
BARGELLO MARKS THE BOOK

I never did finish my bargello belt. After working on it on several occasions but never quite getting it done, I lost it somewhere. And then I realized that I should have started with a smaller-scale project. For your first time out of the gate, it's best to tackle something simple and relatively easy to finish. So maybe save the four-foot-long belt for later—a bookmark will be an easy entrée to the world of bargello needlepoint.

Supplies
Seven-inch by three-inch piece of canvas, yarn in several colors, ribbon that is the same width as the desired width of your bookmark, needlepoint needle, sewing needle, thread

Optional: *Graph paper, colored pencils, fabric pens*

Step One: *Design studio.* Lay out your design on graph paper using colored pencils. You'll use this pattern as your guide when you are in the stitching process. Another option is to mark the beginning of the canvas with some fabric pens and use that to guide your first few stitches. Once those stitches are complete, you can simply continue to repeat their patterns. However, either way you are going to need to count stitches. Be sure to give yourself a cushion of three to four rows of empty canvas on every side. You will need to be able to fold the unstitched canvas over in order to complete your project.

Step Two: *Getting fat yarn through the eye of a needle.* Thread your needle, leaving a little extra yarn doubled over near the eye of the needle. Knot the yarn at the end. Following your paper pattern or mental pattern, bring your yarn up through the canvas and back down again, progressing with each step.

Step Three: *In conclusion.* When you have completed your needlework, it's time to finish the job. Fold the unstitched edges of the canvas over so they lie flat against the back side. At the corners, cut the corner triangle so that when you fold the edges over, the corner fold will be less bulky. Taking your ribbon fancy

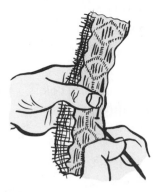

face up, pin it to the back side of your bargello. Using a standard sewing needle and thread in a color that works with your pattern, stitch the ribbon to the back of the canvas. You can stitch the two pieces together using any stitch you like. (Of note: Ribbon is just the suggested backing fabric. If you're in love with a particular fabric and want to use it as your bookmark backing, you certainly can. But to make it easy to work with, you'll want to stitch up the edges of the fabric to give it the already finished quality that a ribbon provides. And stitching it up is another step, and I don't believe in extra steps in a beginner project. Besides, the ribbon looks great on the back. But do what makes you happy!) When your whole canvas piece has been stitched, throw that bad boy in the crease of a book and call it a day.

STITCHERY PROJECT NUMBER TWO:
APPAREL EMBROIDERING

Supplies
T-shirt or other apparel, embroidery floss, embroidery needle, scissors

Optional: *Embroidery hoop, fabric pencil*

While bargello is great, it's certainly not the only needlecraft out there. Sewing is a great skill to have because it extends the life of your clothes and other cloth and I firmly believe in mending things. Although there are undoubtedly plenty of places to buy new clothes in the United States of America today, I have always been a fan of secondhand items. When I was in high school, thrift shopping was out of necessity, but it was also a hobby. I didn't have extra money for new clothes, so I would scour thrift shops trying to find something that would look cool but fit my modest, babysitting-funded budget. I started wearing vintage women's suit jackets that my mother and her mother before her had kept for posterity. It's good to be related to people who save their clothes for posterity.

I loved pairing them with jeans. Looking back, I think I looked pretty sharp. I'm still a huge fan of vintage clothes, and I still love mixing old and new items to give my outfits texture and character. Shopping at secondhand stores takes you back to the whole mantra of eco-friendliness: "Reduce, Reuse, Recycle." Wearing vintage is living the mantra. And while I've been mending clothes for a while, and sometimes begging my expert mother to mend them for me, I have recently discovered the power of restorative embroidery.

A few years back, I got an awesome off-white ladies' woolen undershirt. It's one of these feminine undershirts that appeared in the late '60s/early '70s, with an eyelet sort of design and little puffed sleeves. I had been looking for one for a little while—it was an item that I had seen successfully incorporated into an outfit by a friend, and I was on the hunt for one of my own from the moment I saw it. I finally found one at a flea market in Brooklyn, and I was so excited about my purchase that the very next night I wore it out to a party. And at that party, a friend who shall remain nameless spilled half a glass of red wine down the front of the shirt. We tried to attack the stain immediately, but it was too late. It never came out. I was at a loss for what to do with the shirt. I couldn't bear to part with it, but I couldn't wear it with a red wine stain down the middle. So I shoved it to the back of my dresser drawer, and there it sat for a full calendar year. Then finally, one late winter day, I had a flash of inspiration: "What if I embroidered something over the stain? The stain was long but not wide. I could follow the organic line of the stain and embroider a flower on the shirt!" And that is exactly what I did. I simply covered the stain with freehand stitches. The end result is a super-cute, totally personalized shirt with a cheery blue cornflower right in the middle. Now that I've added the flower, I like it even more than I did before it was stained. And that's saying something.

So, now you know what embroidery has done for me, but what can it do for you? Well, the same thing, silly! You can certainly mark your design on a T-shirt using a fabric pencil beforehand if you prefer to know what your final product is going to look like. For embroidery projects, I always go free-form on the design 'cause that's how I roll. As an Italian guy once said to Rufus's sister, Phoebe: "Me, I have to stay funky." You can use an embroidery hoop to keep your cloth tight and give your hands more protection. And some people even use thimbles. (I've only recently gotten around to buying one of those. It felt like a real sewing milestone for me.) But hoop-full or hoop-less, fingers bare or thimble brandishing, some people call me the space cowboy, some people call me Maurice . . . six of one, half dozen of the other, know what I mean? Just use whatever tools make the crafting more enjoyable for you, and don't worry about what people say. And remember, a few simple stitches can save you a whole lot of dollars and add pop to your wardrobe.

STITCHERY PROJECT NUMBER THREE:
PERSONALIZED NAPKINS

Supplies
Cloth napkins, embroidery floss, embroidery needles, scissors

Optional: *embroidery hoop*

A few chapters back, I suggested that switching to cloth napkins will spare you a lot of needless waste. But, crafter that you are, you don't just want plain old store-bought napkins on your table. So I'm here to tell you how to pump up the cool quotient with your own personal touch, while simultaneously adding a practical

design element. After all, cloth napkins are the best, but if you end up washing them every single time you use them, you'll waste a lot of energy. And wasting energy is no good at all. In a perfect, barbecue-ribs-free world, you should be able to use the same napkin every day for a week. Actually, a perfect world would definitely have barbecued ribs . . . so let me rephrase that. In a perfect world, even the tastiest foods would be only minimally messy, and you would need to wash your cloth napkins only once a week. But in that perfect world, you still want to use your own napkin every time you sit at the table. After all, you don't want to catch cooties from your girlfriend or your kids or your mother-in-law or your houseguest. A little stitchery will make your napkins stand out from one another.

If you want to keep it simple, you can embroider the initials of your household regulars on the corner of each napkin. For guest napkins, try embroidering "Our Guest" on the corner. Planning to have more than one guest? Embroider "Our Guest" in different but complementary colors. For a slightly subtler signifier, you can choose a favorite image and embroider that onto the cloth. Simple designs can be funny. You can do opposites: cats and dogs; suns and moons; flames and waves; angels and devils; tortoises and hares. Or go with a theme: vegetables, cars, flowers, traffic signs—whatever floats your boat. And choose a napkin in a dark color so that tiny little stains don't appear as monster stains. After all, even if your friends and family are into ecology, they might be a little grossed out by obvious stains from last night's dinner. Any way you tackle it, the needlework you do this Crafternoon is sure to add something fun to your home or your wardrobe.

CHAPTER SEVEN

FREEDOM CRAFT!

*I hold these truths to be self-evident, that all Crafters are created equal,
that they are endowed with certain unalienable Rights . . . that among
these are Life, Liberty, and the pursuit of Craftiness.*

—EXCERPT FROM *THE DECLARATION OF CRAFTERNOON,* A.D. 2007

Crafternoon should always be a celebration of freedom of expression and a manifestation of the joys of liberty. That's why I always invite Crafternoon participants to bring their own craft projects to the 'noon, no matter what the overarching theme is. But in this month of liberty celebrating, make individual expression a mandate! In the Declaration of Independence, signed on July 4, 1776, Thomas Jefferson declares that: "When a long train of abuses and usurpations, pursuing invariably the same Object evinces a design to reduce them [the people] under absolute Despotism, it is their [the people's] right, it is their [the people's] duty, to throw off such Government, and to provide new Guards for their future security." Say it, T. Jefferson! Tell it to the despots! We're not going to take it anymore. We celebrate our free will with a Freedom Craft!

E veryone shall bring his or her own craft project to this Craft-ernoon, so that we can engage and inspire one another with surprising new-to-you crafts. I issue this new charter for your July Crafternoon:

Let the people of Crafternoon craft freely, without theme or design, so that they might pursue the craft of their choice, such that they may be unified in their individuality and inspired by the introduction of heretofore unknown crafts. Let them pledge to explore the bound-aries of their craft abilities and to support one another in the crafting process. Prudence, indeed, will dictate that the Freedom Crafternoon shall breathe excitement into the Crafternoon year and shall leave the people invigorated and filled with new enthusiasm for the free-wheeling side of crafting. This pledge of crafting freedom shall act as a guide for all future Crafternoons and shall serve as a reminder that crafting is an experience that exalts the individual while unifying the community. This I solemnly declare, with liberty and crafting for all.

—Excerpt from the pamphlet
"Common Sense for Freedom Craft," A.D. 2007

July is the height of picnic season, so take your Crafternoon outdoors and have yourself a crafty little picnic. Crafternoon hosts who have backyards can celebrate the great outdoors just outside their door. City dwellers like me can seek out a good spot in a great park, ideally one with a big tree to dwell under for those who fear overexposure to the bright sunlight. And if you're a coastal kid, you could even host a Crafternoon beach party! Although you won't have access to all of your usual craft supplies (unless you're in your backyard) and you may not even have a table to work on, you'll have nature, the best craft supply of all.

When I hosted my Freedom Craft picnic, the projects brought by the crafters were quite varied. My friend Marie and her daughter Madeline brought a beading kit and made some cool beaded necklaces. My mom brought a knitting project that she wanted to finish up. My friend Ryan brought a stamp of an eyeball and a stamp pad, and basically just stamped the heck out of everything he saw. My friend Judson came along with his friends Kate and Elliot, and they were also working on making jewelry. My friend Jen swung by with her mom for the picnic portion and just crafted up some witty banter to share with our friends. And me? I was knitting a baby hat to have on hand for a TBD baby. It's always good to have a baby gift on hand, and a baby hat is a small, easy-to-carry craft project. It was fun just to sit on a blanket and enjoy the company of other crafters, each one doing his or her own thing but living together in harmony.

OF CRAFT I SING, BABY

So this Crafternoon is all about freedom, but perhaps you're looking for a little inspiration to get into the spirit. Of all of the famous figures in the American Revolution, who is the craftiest? If you guessed George Washington, that's weird, and you should see me after class. If you guessed Betsy Ross, you just earned yourself a gold star. Yes, Betsy Ross is the American Revolution's Craft General. Credited with making the first American flag, she plays the female lead in discussions of the Revolution. And while she wasn't out on the field of battle, she did something very revolutionary—using a needle and thread, she created a crafty voice of change.

(By the way, I know I said this was a Freedom Craft, so you can skip the next few pages if you don't want to hear my suggestions for this 'noon. I'm not trying to get all Establishment on you; I'm just offering some options.)

GET THE WORD OUT AND SET UP YOUR SPACE

How do you gather your picnic people? Send them an email that goes a little something like this:

> Hello, my crafty people! This Saturday, please join me for a late-afternoon Freedom Craft Crafternoon! From 2 p.m. to 6 p.m. in the park we will be crafting whatever we feel like in the company of friends.
>
> This is a free-for-all, so you are encouraged to bring a craft project that you've been meaning to start or to finish. My mom will be there to answer craft questions that might come up. She is very good at helping a craft project along if it's reached a bump in its craft road, as well as just giving a little love and support. If you want to try something new, I'll have some projects on hand to test your crafty mettle.
>
> Please feel free to bring a treat of the savory or the sweet variety to be shared with your fellow crafters. Tasty beverages are also a good addition to any Crafternoon. And bring something to sit on! It's more fun to craft when you're feeling comfy.
>
> If you think of it, RSVP to me! And pass the invitation along to crafty boys and girls who might be interested in attending. And hey, that means crafty moms and dads and daughters and sons and sisters and brothers and spiritual advisers, too!

Supplies (All supplies are optional—I'm not trying to stomp on your Freedom)
Felt, thread, needles, straight pins, good scissors, a book, construction paper or posterboard, old magazines, old books, old newspapers, glue sticks, contact paper, magnetic sheets or magnetic tape

Now that you've notified the masses and checked on your supplies, you want to pack a tasty treat that is compact and not terribly perishable. How about a delicious bean and pesto spread? I think you'll find that this is just the right addition to your crafty gathering.

TREAT OF THE 'NOON:
Bean and Pesto Spread

One 15-ounce can white beans
½ cup olive oil
¼ cup pine nuts
2 cloves garlic, pressed
¼ cup grated Parmesan cheese
1 cup fresh basil, coarsely chopped
Splash of lemon juice

Drain and rinse the beans, then put them in a food processor. Add the olive oil, pine nuts, garlic, Parmesan, and basil. Purée until the spread reaches a smooth consistency. Add a splash of lemon juice. Serve with pita chips or bagel chips.

FREEDOM PROJECT NUMBER ONE:
FLY YOUR CRAFT FLAG

Supplies
Felt in multiple colors, thread in contrasting colors, needle, straight pins, scissors

Why not pay tribute to Ms. Ross by sewing yourself your own Crafternoon flag? You can hang it in a window when your Crafters are coming over, or you can fly it outside your door day and night. And the next time you have a Crafternoon picnic, you can tell your friends to look for the flag flying high above your blanket. The flag will be a symbol of what Crafternoon means to you. There are so many ways to go with this, so let your mind run free. I'm a simple girl, so when I made mine I simply chose my favorite craft tools and collaged their silhouettes together to make a cool image of crafting craziness. I use some crazy felt colors so the flag really pops. And you don't have to stop there. You could make a checkerboard on the back of your flag so the flag becomes a dual-functioning object. When your craft flag wasn't flying, you could take it down and use it to play some checkers.

Step One: *No, I never felt like this before.* Hit your nearest fabric or art-supply store for a wide range of fabric options. You can choose to work with any fabric you like, but I'm feeling felt. Felt is really easy to work with because it's so stiff. Cutting a shape in felt is a total breeze. And something about it reminds me of kindergarten. It's got an innocent feel to it. Of course, you can always skip the stores altogether and just fabric dive in your own supply closet. In fact, that might make the final product even more interesting.

Step Two: *The pitter-patter of pretty patterns.* If you're a whiz with scissors, go ahead and cut your patterns freehand. I can easily freehand a heart or a square, but if I try to cut a design any more complicated than that, the end result is going to be unidentifiable. And while abstract expressionism is always cool, I want a touch of realism in my symbolic flag. So I'd trace my desired image onto a piece of paper. After the tracing is complete, I'd cut the image out of the paper and pin it to my fabric of choice, then grab my scissors to make the final cut. This step can be repeated for each image you plan to appliqué onto your flag.

Step Three: *Because I said sew.* Once you've got your felt pieces cut out, start arranging them on your flag. When you've settled on placement, pin each piece to the background with a straight pin. Sew the appliquéd pieces on by hand. I recommend using a running stitch, and sewing with a contrasting but complementary thread color. First, cut a 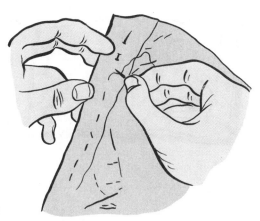 piece of thread long enough to stretch from your hand to about the middle of your chest. Thread your needle, pulling a little extra thread through the needle so the thread doesn't slip, then make a double knot at the bottom of your thread. The running stitch is very simple: It looks like the dotted line in the middle of a road. Start with your needle on the underside of your flag, then bring it up through the layers of fabric and then back down through the layers again. Try to make the space between each stitch even. Repeat until you have secured your image. Tie a neat double knot at the end of your work as close to the felt as possible and then snip the thread near the knot.

Finish the top or the left side of the flag with a tubular seam to accommodate your stick or the string you'll be hoisting your flag with. Simply fold over your fabric and sew a straight running stitch along the outside edge of the fold, making sure you do not sew up either end of the seam. Insert a pole and, voilà, you have a flag!

FREEDOM PROJECT NUMBER TWO:
PRESS ME ON IT

I was in a bookstore recently and discovered a very old composition book that was practically blank, with the exception of a few pages of scientific formulas. But in every other page of the notebook, there was a different pressed leaf or flower. They were lodged in the binding of the book, hidden away like pressed secrets. I had forgotten all about pressed things and how cool they can look, so the book reminded me how beautiful they are and what a perfect outdoor project flower and leaf pressing is. So take some time out of your freedom day to scout for leaves and flowers. You want to find the best specimens out there to press. Remember, if something is brown when you pluck it, it will remain brown when it dries. And if it's red when it's plucked, red it shall remain, albeit a slightly faded red. That's a nice thing about pressing—it preserves so much of the essence of the item being pressed.

Supplies
Leaves or flowers, big books, scissors

Step One: *Locate and pluck the pressee.* Since you're already outdoors, what better time to look for live, pressable items. You'll find that leaves lend themselves to pressing more than flowers because, generally, they are already flat. The dimensions of the average flower make it difficult to press—a pressed rose wouldn't work very well since it's thick. A pressed copper beech leaf, on the other hand, would look just lovely. If you insist on using flowers, pansies are the perennial favorite of the pressed-flower world because they are delicate and colorful and surprisingly flat.

Once you have found your floral or foliage muse, pluck it from its perch using clean, sharp scissors. Cut the fresh flower or leaf down to the size you want to see it when it is pressed—don't leave a lot of extra stem and plan to cut it after it dries. When it is dry, it will be far more delicate and a snip from your scissors may cause it to crumble. I recommend cutting it close and clean, like a preppy haircut.

Step Two: *Press it!* Using a book with blank pages, lay your leaf or flower flat on the page. If you have kept the stem long, you can pose the stem in a swoop, in a curl, in a figure eight—whatever your heart desires. Then close the book on it. Give it a few weeks, years, or decades to dry and then incorporate it into a future craft project. Preservation rocks!

GREAT MOMENTS IN CRAFT HISTORY: *The Invention of the Glue Stick*

Until sometime in the 1970s or '80s, glue had been available only in liquid form. As a liquid, it served its basic adhesive purpose but could prove to be difficult to manage when making a nice collage. With the advent of the glue stick, crafters the world over rejoiced. This cunning new invention allowed glue to be applied in a controlled fashion. How smoothly it glides across the paper, leaving neither bumps nor bubbles in its aftermath! How nicely it remains within its compact little tube, never straying to make its mark on woolen pants and children's hair! How efficiently it is applied to each corner of a page, without the issue of overgluing! In my opinion, no paper-heavy Crafternoon should be without a serious stockpile of glue sticks. In fact, no crafty home is complete without glue sticks. Glue sticks are to Crafternoon as rolls of duct tape are to MacGyver—without them, impossible tasks remain impossible. But with a glue stick and a little ingenuity, you can rescue almost any Crafternoon project *and* get the girl.

FREEDOM CRAFT PROJECT NUMBER THREE:
MAGNETIC FIELDS

To draw more folks to your crafting idyll, what better tool than the magnet! At some point in 2003, I went through a short but passionate magnet-making phase. My love of old magazines knows no bounds, but after valentine making and decoupaging and decorating my room, I started running out of things to do with all of my cool, clipped images. When I finally thought of magnet making, my stockpile of vintage images had a new purpose.

I love a fridge crowded with photographs and posters and flyers from friends' shows and postcards and the odd real estate listing cut out by my dad and marked "CHEAP! LOVE, DAD." Therefore, I need a lot of magnets. Once I'd come up with the idea to make my own, I had to figure out a way to make my magnets stick. I adhered the images to posterboard, then covered the image completely in contact paper, which effectively laminates the paper and also strengthens it. I generally used good old-fashioned magnetic tape, but you can also buy magnetic sheets that you can cut down to any size you choose.

Supplies
Old magazines, books, newspapers, or photos, construction paper or posterboard for your background (you'll definitely need poster-board if you opt for magnetic tape over magnetic sheets), glue stick, contact paper, scissors, magnetic sheets or tape

Optional: chopsticks

Step One: *Cut it out and stick it on.* Cut out some magnet-size images from magazines, newspapers, old books, or photos. (You could also draw your own designs directly on posterboard and use them as your images.) You could search for some patriotic symbols like eagles and American flags to honor the Freedom Craft theme. If you are using posterboard, cut it to your desired size. Then use a glue stick or other clear glue on the back of the image, and adhere it to the posterboard. If you're using magnetic sheets, you don't have to use posterboard for sturdiness; you can glue the image directly onto the magnetic sheet. You're so good at this!

Step Two: *Cover it up.* Next, cut a piece of contact paper exactly the same size and shape as your posterboard backing or magnetic sheet. Place the contact paper sticky side up and remove the protective sheet. (Maybe it goes without saying that the contact paper should be sticky side up. After all, we're making magnets, not contact-covered tabletops. But I like to be thorough.) Care-fully place your paper collage facedown on the sticky side of the contact paper, pressing firmly. Pick up the magnet carefully by the corners to check that there are no air bubbles. If there are bub-bles, place the magnet on the table and use chopsticks to force any air bubbles from the center out to the sides.

Step Three: *Magnetism!* If you're using magnetic tape, cut a piece of it to the appropriate length and adhere it to the back of the contact-sealed image. Now you've got a working magnet. If you decided to use the magnetic sheet instead, go slap your new magnet on your fridge and see how purdy she looks.

As a crafty side note, my best friend Christine also started making magnets when we were roommates in Brooklyn. When she got hitched to the wonderful John in 2006, she made j'adorable souvenir magnets for all of her wedding guests. Here's how. She cut a magnet to be just slightly larger than the image she was working with, then adhered a piece of colored paper to the front side of the magnet with a glue stick, leaving a little lip around the edge (you could cut it to the exact size if you prefer). She typed the location and date of the wedding on white paper and cut out the words. She then overlaid the date and location on an old magazine image of a couple in love. She finished it all off with a piece of contact paper cut to size and adhered it directly to the front. Now every time I see her homemade magnet on my fridge, I think of how much I adore my best friend and how fun her beautiful wedding day was. When was the last time a magnet evoked so much emotion in you?

Whether you choose to fly your craft flag, press flowers into your service, make yourself something magnetic, or choose a project of your own design, this celebration of crafty freedom is sure to make for a fun summer day. And fun should certainly be included in our list of unalienable rights.

CHAPTER EIGHT

AUGUST

WHEN A PROBLEM COMES AROUND, YOU MUST QUILT IT!

Quilts—they're not just for the Amish anymore! In the old days, they were found mainly in New England cottages, or covering the mattresses at sleepy bed-and-breakfasts, or hanging in my parents' apartment. But they have recently burst onto the bedcover scene. They are hot! Quilts are everywhere, showing up in fancy interior-design magazines and even making their way into the modern art world. Quilts are the "It" girls of the bedcover set.

What makes a quilt, you ask? It's defined as a bedcovering made up of three layers—the backing, the warm, chewy center, and the decorative top. Americans certainly didn't invent quilting, but they made it pop with piecing. Colonists could not afford to waste any material whatsoever, so reusing everything was a way of life. Piecing together scraps of fabric to make quilt tops began as a necessary evil and evolved into an art form. Colonial life was rough, and although we're living better now, recycling is making news and gaining new friends, so what better time to get back to quilting? The American contribution to this ancient craft was a symbol of American thrift and ingenuity, and that makes it both cool and totally relevant. So I figured I'd do some research and start planning a Quilting Crafternoon for August. I know no one really needs a quilt in August unless they live someplace chilly, but quilting is a complex craft and requires some extra time. With September's crisp fall evenings just around the corner, August seemed like the perfect time to get quilting.

To get into the quilting frame of mind, I went to Soho to check out Purl Patchwork. My friend Mitch had recommended it months earlier, and I finally got a free afternoon to pay a visit. From the moment I laid eyes on the big picture window, I realized this store was going to be trouble. I walked through the glass door into the clean, narrow space, and I was instantly, madly in love. Every bolt of fabric called out to me: "Maura! Look at me! I'm a copy of a popular *seed catalog* print from the 1930s! I am quaint and I am printed in a lovely old-fashioned red! Hey, Maura, look over here! I'm a modern kids' print of elephants and other animals, and I'm not afraid to make the bold and intelligent move of combining pink and brown!"

I walked slowly through the store, pulling out every other bolt to drool over the gorgeous designs. The inventory was a mixture of totally modern fabric and reprints of the most beautiful, nostalgic old designs. There wasn't a fabric ugly duckling in the whole wide bunch. But I managed to exercise some serious willpower. When I was ready to leave the store, I walked up to the cash register with only three yards of glorious fabric in hand. "Wow," I marveled to myself, "I'm going to make it out of this store for cheap! I am thrifty!" My fabric was packed up, the credit card was charged, I signed my name on the dotted line, and I was about to ease on down the road. But then a piece of paper caught my eye. It read, Quilt Making by Hand with Cassandra. I stopped dead in my tracks and read on.

Turns out the store offers a class where students can learn how to hand quilt in four two-hour classes. At the time, I didn't know all that much about quilting. I was interested in it, but I had never had my very own quilting Crafternoon. It was the one major craft that I was curious about that I had yet to tackle. I had figured I would read some books about quilting and ask some quilters for some quick lessons and then I would basically teach myself how to do it. After all, that's how I've done most Crafternoons when I didn't have an expert handy—I did some research and I gave it a go. In a thrift store, I'd already found a great old book on quilting called *The Mountain Artisans Quilting Book* by Alfred Allan Lewis with loads of awesome step-by-step instructions accompanied by great black-and-white photos of quilts in the process of being created. (It's also got its fair share of hand drawn designs and some amazing pictures of Sharon Rockefeller in some butt-kicking floor-length quilted skirts.) But after I tried my hand at my first prototype— the quilted earring—I started thinking that it would help to have a little living guidance. I had definitely learned from my unguided quilting adventure, but I figured it couldn't hurt to get some pointers from a real-deal quilter. So I asked the lady ringing up my fabric if there was still space available in the class. She said there were only two spots left. I knew I had to act fast, so my credit card came back out of hiding. Gee, it's hard to be thrifty.

And just who do you think filled that last empty spot? Well, after I signed up for the class, I immediately started gushing to my mom about how awesome the store was and how I was going to have to drag her there on a field trip right away and how I had signed up for a really cool quilting class. "Oh, the class sounds like fun," she said, in a way that someone says, "Oh, the party sounds like fun," when she hasn't been invited to the party but she so totally wants to go. Quilting is also one of the few crafts that my mother has yet to tackle. My mother and I have never taken a class together, though we always thought it would be seriously fun. "You should take the class with me!" I yelled. She said yes instantaneously, and before you could say batting, I had called the store and signed her up for the class. Yes, the last two spots went to the Madden Ladies.

The very next week, we were off on our four-week quilting class adventure. Taking the class was like attending a miniversion of Crafternoon once a week that I didn't need to organize. Of course, it was kind of hilarious to see the different approaches my mom and I took to the class and to the craft. My mom was amazing about always doing her homework—she pieced together almost ten squares, while I felt triumphant to have completed just two and a half. Her sewing was meticulous, and her squares were perfectly ironed. My stitches were small but inconsistent, and I always had to borrow the store iron. She did a patch test on her red fabric to make sure it wouldn't bleed. I just hoped for the best with my red-and-white fabric. The last class, I had forgotten completely to bring a key supply—the awkwardly named "fat quarters." Most quilting shops sell these in little bins somewhere in the store—they are usually pieces of fabric approximately 18 inches by 22 inches. My mother was there with several fat quarters and a roll of pictures she had taken of our family quilts. She made me look bad, but I loved her for it.

The teacher, Cassandra, taught us all of the basics—how to design your quilting squares, how to cut your templates, how to piece the pieces together. I had looked at the template-making process in the book, but I had decided against actually making templates because it was a step that was too time-consuming for my taste. I'm definitely a fan of immediate gratification, and I was more interested in cutting the fabrics and sewing them together than I was in the multistep template process. I figured that I would just always cut squares that fit together to form other squares and be done with it. But in the class, I found out that by using graph paper, you can draw other shapes like triangles and squares in the middle of squares, shapes that will even come together to make a square. And that's pretty cool.

It was a lot of work to create patterns with a ruler using graph paper, then cut plastic templates, then use those templates to cut pieces, then pin the pieces together to make quilting squares. So it was good to have Cassandra standing right there to show us what to do because I didn't want to give up on the process half-way through. Cassandra was basically my quilting personal trainer.

I enjoyed myself in the first three classes, but I felt slightly over-whelmed by the pattern making and sewing-along-straight-lines-by-hand. I finally blossomed when it came time to quilt. I got that hoop in my hand and got my batting-and-fat-quarters sandwich secured in the hoop, and then I started quilting. And that's when it clicked. Stitching the light blue outline of a baby elephant free-hand, I knew I had turned a corner in my quilting life. And just when I thought it couldn't get any better, Cassandra broke out a whole cloth quilt that she'd been working on. The entire quilt is made from just three pieces: the top, the batting, and the bottom. The top and the bottom are both cut from the whole cloth—no piecing involved. And with needle and thread, Cassandra was in the process of drawing an intricate design masterpiece. It was the purest example of quilting I had ever seen. Looking at that whole-cloth quilt, I knew then that I had found my quilty calling. Pieced quilts look amazing, but the process doesn't suit my personality. I like to live life in the crafting fast lane. When you're making a whole-piece quilt, you're doing 150 on the crafty autobahn.

QUIZ TIME! WHAT KIND OF A QUILT LOVER ARE YOU?

Take This Simple Quiz and Find Out How to Turn Up the Heat in Bed—By Using a Quilt!

My idea of a dream vacation is:

A. *Lying on a beach drinking piña coladas*

B. *Hiking in the wilderness with nothing but a compass to guide me*

C. *Sitting by a lake with a good book*

D. *Organizing electronic files*

My signature meal is:

A. *Steak on the grill and some fine red wine*

B. *A complete macrobiotic meal served with a hot cup of twig tea*

C. *Roast chicken and homemade apple pie*

D. *Overcooked ramen noodles*

My dream vehicle is:

A. *A high-speed motorboat, equipped with a cooler of brewskies*

B. *A foldaway bicycle*

C. *A minivan*

D. *The Internet*

My favorite song is:
- A. *"Margaritaville" by Jimmy Buffett*
- B. *"Peace Train" by Cat Stevens*
- C. *"God Bless America" by Irving Berlin*
- D. *"Computer Love" by Kraftwerk*

When I sleep, I dream of:
- A. *Dancing beer bottles*
- B. *World peace*
- C. *Playing one last game with the ghosts of legendary baseball players in a cornfield*
- D. *Electric sheep*

If you chose A for three or more questions, you are a fun-loving, life-embracing person. You also might have an alcohol problem. I'm not saying, I'm just saying. I mean, every A answer involves alcohol. So, think about that. As a quilter, you will be drawn to simple, easy-to-make quilting projects that provide almost instant gratification. Like a Long Island Iced Tea but in quilt form. But the nice thing about quilting is that unlike a real Long Island Iced Tea, your quilted projects will never leave you with regrets. The projects herein should do you right.

If you chose answer B for three or more questions, you are a hippie. Would it kill you to stop burning the patchouli incense? I realize that you're trying to cover up the smell of other types of, ahem, smoke, but it smells like a slap in the face. As a quilter you display a slow and sloppy technique, which you prefer to refer to as "organic." You're willing to try any project, as long as The Man isn't going to stick his nose in your business and make you follow some dumb rules. Guess what? We're the same style! Yeah! But please note: I do *not* burn patchouli.

If you chose C for three or more questions, you are a patriotic, family-oriented quilter. You're on the PTA, you bake goodies every other night, and you love to craft. As a quilter, you will be diligent and follow patterns. You may even be frustrated by my lack of instructions for a full-sized quilt, and you may tsk-tsk to yourself when you are done with this chapter, wondering why in the world I would call it quilting when you don't learn how to make a quilt! But then you discover that the next chapter is about clay, and you'll remember how much you used to love those California raisin commercials, and you'll recall that those raisins were made of clay, and you'll give me another chance.

If you chose D for three or more questions, you are so not the target audience for this book. Please don't take that the wrong way—I'm really glad you bought it! You are a techie, and you love nothing more than sitting in front of your computer for hours on end, not seeing the sun for weeks at a time. Seriously, your skin is starting to turn translucent, that's how pale you are. But you were drawn to crafting. You want your flesh to touch cloth and that cloth to be touched by a needle and thread. You want something real, not virtual. As a quilter, you will be drawn to complex projects that can be worn as costumes to Comic Con. Did somebody say Quilted Storm Trooper Costume? Yes, somebody did. And that somebody is you.

GET THE WORD OUT AND SET UP YOUR SPACE

Crafternoon is just a modern-day quilting bee, except we don't always quilt and we don't always drink lemonade. For some reason, I can't imagine a quilting bee without imagining a huge pitcher of lemonade somewhere nearby. So let's make some lemonade with a Crafternoon twist . . . make it a Half & Half, Connecticut's state beverage. No, wait, that's the Gin & Tonic. I give you Connecticut's second most popular beverage, the Half & Half.

But before I hit you with this thirst-quenching recipe, I ought to set the scene for you and your crafters-to-be. So read on, and if you behave yourself, you just might get a bonus recipe.

It's August, and it's hot as all get-out there on the street. So why not come in out of the haze and craft an afternoon away? This month we'll tackle the techniques of quilting, a craft that leads to cozy bedcovers if you can muster up enough patience.

If you're interested in making some place mats, bring along the following materials: fabric-cutting scissors, at least one yard of fabric, sewing needle, standard good-quality cotton thread. If you feel like creating a quilty little wall hanging, bring two 12-inch by 12-inch squares of fabric, a 12-inch by 12-inch square of batting, six feet of ribbon, and a thimble. And if you want to beautify your face with some earrings, bring along some fabric scraps, craft pliers, head pins, and fishhook earrings.

If you want to learn the skills of template making, you should also grab some template plastic (available at most fabric stores) and scissors to cut plastic. I'll provide some graph paper, pencils, and rulers.

If all those materials make your head spin, just bring yourself and any craft project you like. And we always love foodie and drinkish donations, so feel free to contribute something for consumption. I'm looking forward to hitting the fabric with you.

xoxo,

Maura

Still thirsty? Me, too! Well turn the page already! And you, you behaved very nicely. You won the bonus. Give yourself a high five and make yourself some lemon squares to celebrate.

THE ELEMENTS OF QUILTING STYLE

There are two primary elements that go into making a quilt: piecing and quilting. Each can exist independent of the other. While many of us think of quilts simply as the calico-cloth, log-cabin-design mega-bedcovers, a log-cabin design does not a quilt make. As an amateur quilter, I am more interested in exploring the elements than I am in tackling a quilt. So rather than act as if I know more than I actually do, I'll simply explain what I do know.

Maybe you've got a favorite shirt that has been patched and repatched so many times that there's barely anything left of it.

TREAT OF THE 'NOON, BEVERAGE EDITION:
The Half & Half

4 decaf black tea bags
7 ½ cups water
1 cup fresh-squeezed lemon juice (6–8 lemons)
½ cup sugar
Sprigs of fresh mint (optional)

In a large pitcher, add the tea bags to 4 cups of water. Put it in the refrigerator to brew for at least 2 hours. In another pitcher, mix the lemon juice with 3 cups of water. In a bowl, stir the sugar and ½ cup of water together until it takes on a syrupy quality. Then add the sugar water to the water and lemon mixture. Taste and add additional sugar as desired. Add the lemonade to the iced tea and mix it on up. For extra pizzazz, add a few sprigs of fresh mint, and muddle at the bottom of the pitcher. Serve over ice.

Could you finally retire it from your wardrobe if you knew that it would be reborn as part of a quilt? I think you could. Now if you're a hoarding crafter who, like me, believes in scrap preservation, you might not need to make those kinds of cut-shirt decisions. I've got bags and drawers stuffed to capacity with a wide variety of odd scraps. Either way, you don't need to go to the fabric store to find the perfect bolt of cotton cloth and the most complementary thread to sew it with. (I'm not saying you *can't* do that—of course you can.) But you can make something just as sturdy, just as interesting, and just as warm if you mine your own closet for material.

TREAT OF THE 'NOON, FOOD EDITION:
Lemon Hip-to-Be-Squares

2½ cups flour
½ pound butter, room temperature
½ cup plus 1 tablespoon confectioners' sugar
4 eggs
2 cups granulated sugar
½ teaspoon salt
6 tablespoons lemon juice
Grated zest of 1 lemon

Preheat the oven to 350°F. In a large mixing bowl, cream together the 2 cups of flour, the butter, and ½ cup of the confectioners' sugar. Press the mixture into the bottom of an ungreased 9 x 13-inch Pyrex pan until it's firm like an athlete's abs. Bake for 15 minutes.

In a bowl, mix the eggs, granulated sugar, and salt. Then blend in the lemon juice and zest. Sift the remaining ½ cup of flour and 1 tablespoon confectioners' sugar into the egg mixture and fold in. Pour over the crust and bake for another 30 minutes. Take the pan out of the oven, and sift additional confectioners' sugar over the top like it's a sugar blizzard. Loosen the edges with a knife. Cut when cool.

CRAFTY INTERLUDE:
Practice Makes ~~Perfect~~ Better

Hey there, Perfectionists! How are you today? Oh, how silly of me to ask. I should *know*—you're perfect! Tackled any new craft projects lately? Oh, of course you have—you were talking about teaching yourself smocking with hand-dyed embroidery floss on linen you wove with your very own nimble hands. How is that going for you? Right, it's great. I should have guessed as much. Everything is always great for you.

How am *I* doing? Oh, I'm really good. Yeah, I'm trying to make myself these teeny-tiny quilted earrings, and I know they're going to look great, but damn it, they're making me nuts! See, I'm sort of just vibing it out with the earrings. No pattern, just a poorly laid out plan. The first one I tried to make, I sewed the backing and the front pieces together from the outside, forgetting all about the basic sewing technique of seaming fabric together and then turning it inside out so the seam disappears. So the first one looks totally sloppy. And I don't have a thimble, so I keep stabbing myself with the needle when I misfire, which makes me kind of cranky.

Oh, and then I tried to do the second earring, and this time I *did* remember to sew the pieces together so the outsides faced each other for maximum seam-hiding action. But when I flipped the thing inside out, the corners were all lumpy and weird. I kept trying to pull them out to make them come to a point, but it never really worked—the corners just wouldn't pop. When I was reading a book later in the day, it mentioned that one should cut the triangle of fabric at the corner just past the seam before turning the piece inside out, and that technique should make the corners pop right out. I had completely forgotten about the triangle cut! It made so much sense.

Now I'm going for prototype number three, and I'm feeling pretty good about this one, though I have to figure out how to get the batting inside the earring. I'll admit that I was getting slightly frustrated when I was tackling that first prototype. Scratch that—I was getting pissed. In retrospect, it's super silly getting pissed over a tiny quilted earring. I like to imagine what I looked like as I stabbed away at those tiny cloth squares, getting madder by the minute, the thought bubble in my head reading, "I hate this tiny friggin' quilt!" I couldn't figure out why I wasn't able to get things to work. At one point, Rufus walked in as I was mid-huff and looked at me with a mixture of empathy and amusement. I think my face was contorted in a particularly uncomfortable expression. He just looked at me and said, "Maura, you have to enjoy the process!" What a simple but powerful reminder, eh, Perfectionist? That sentence deserves to be in bold: **Enjoy the process!**

Reminding myself of that really helped. But then I stuck myself with that sharp little needle and got mad all over again. So Rufus reminded me that that's part of the reason why I like to learn new things at Crafternoon, in a group setting, 'cause learning in a group is just a lot more fun. Man, it's handy to have a Rufus! You just can't get as annoyed at yourself and your own clumsiness when your friends are around because if you do get annoyed, chances are you'll get called out on it and you'll just have to laugh it off. That's assuming your friends have a sense of humor about things. If they don't, you need to get a new group of friends. Look me up when you come to New York and we'll hang out.

By the time I was done with the second prototype, I was pretty happy with my still-sloppy-but-increasingly-less-sloppy results. I know those earrings are getting better looking each time I make a new pair of them, and I'm just happy to know that I'm learning something new with each new version. You know what they say: "Practice makes better!"

Wait, where are you going, Perfectionist? Did I say something to offend you? Oh, I didn't realize "practice makes **perfect**" was your official motto! Well, I wouldn't say that I *butchered* it . . . more like updated it. Look, Perfectionist, I'm not trying to make you mad. I'm just trying to address the people out there who are less concerned about perfection and more concerned about getting better at what they are doing. The people like me who really love learning new things, but whose ultimate goal in life isn't perfection—it's experience. I wasn't trying to offend you. I admire your work ethic. And the craft projects you produce are always beautiful. I hope you'll forgive me, Perfectionist. I'm just trying to create my own type of person. Instead of Perfectionists, we'll be Better-ers. Better-er: noun, a person who demands more of himself, herself, or others. Yeah, that's not perfect, but it's more better.

BACK TO THE ELEMENTS OF QUILTING STYLE

As I was saying, I like learning about what makes a quilt a quilt. Luckily for curious little me, my parents bought some quilts dirt cheap back in the 1970s, and they have generously given me a couple of these cool quilts to use on my very own bed. The quilt that I have on my bed right now is pretty old; there are a few places here and there where the fabric has worn out. I've been meaning to repair it because I don't want the damage to get worse. But I'm going to hold off on that a little longer because those damage points are the places where I can see its inner workings. It's a bold display of the quilt's guts—the flip side of the backing, the batting, and the underbelly of the fronting. Stitches show their true colors in these little quilt wounds, so I sit and stare at it, gently pulling the layers apart. Then I refer back to *The Mountain Artisans Quilting Book,* and I start getting my head around the how of quilting. It's given me a good sense of what quilts are all about.

I don't want to be credited for starting a movement of folks running around attics looking for quilts and then giddily pulling them apart. Don't pull things apart! Pristine examples of crafting goodness shouldn't just be hacked to pieces like a teenager on a date at Make-Out Point. But if they have damage already, you can look and see what they've got going on. There's a lot you can learn from just looking at something from the outside. Try to get your hands on a real, live example of the thing you want to get crafting, in good condition or bad. Holding it in your hands and studying it is going to make a world of difference. Trust me, Leonardo would totally agree.

PIECING IT TOGETHER

So, quilting is a lot of work. A LOT of work. Are you ready to go whole hog into the world of full-sized quilt making? I'll tell you this much—I thought I was, and I am definitely not. To decide on the projects for this chapter, my mom and I had a mini-Crafternoon where we went over our notes from the quilting class and tried to figure out what projects would be best to share with the world. We decided on a few things:

1. It is unlikely that either one of us will ever make a full-sized quilt.

2. Basting seems annoying.

Having made those two decisions, we were ready to lay out the following steps for aspiring quilters.

QUILTING BASICS:
DRAFTING, PIECING, AND QUILTING

There are three techniques that are the cornerstones of quilt making: drafting, piecing, and quilting. Drafting is not as intimidating as it sounds. I'm not shipping you off to architecture school; I'm just asking you to pick up a little graph paper. When you are drafting for quilting projects, you are simply making a pattern or template that you can use over and over when you are cutting pieces for your quilts. Drafting helps you cut pieces that are the same size every time and ensures that the pieces will fit together to form a proper square. You want your square to be proper, don't you? Of course you do—you're a very proper crafter! So here are the basic steps to drafting your quilt pieces:

Supplies
Graph paper, sharp pencil with eraser, ruler, template plastic (available at most fabric stores), scissors to cut plastic

Step One: *Find your pattern.* Using a ruler and the boxes on your graph paper as your guide, you will be able to draft any pattern. Decide how big you'd like your square to be. Then, using your ruler, draw a square of the desired size on the graph paper, following the lines to make sure you stay straight. Unless you are using graph paper specifically designed for drafting quilting patterns (yes, such a thing exists), give yourself a margin around the edge of the paper before you start drawing. Graph paper gets a little wonky around the edges, so you want to make sure you're drawing and measuring on full squares. If you are doing a simple pattern like a foursquare, you simply need to draw your large square and then divide it into quarters with lines. Give each section a letter: A, B, C, and D. And please note that when you are drawing your lines, go heavy on the pencil—you'll need to be able to see it through the template plastic.

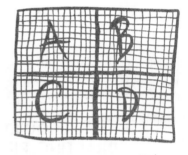

Step Two: *Lay your template plastic over the graph paper.* Using your ruler to keep you in line, trace the lines of each section of the square onto the template plastic. The template plastic is transparent, which allows this magical tracing to occur. Don't trace each piece right next to the other—give yourself at least ½ inch of space between pieces. In the center of each template piece, write the corresponding letter. (This helps you to keep track of what you're working on and also makes the plastic more visible and therefore less easy to lose.) You can also draw arrows to indicate which sides of the template pieces create the outside edges of your squares. That helps when you are piecing the fabric together to make your squares.

Carefully cut out your template pieces and mark them. It's a good idea to keep all of the template pieces for one square in the same place. So, for example, if you have a square that is made up of four triangles, you would keep all four triangular template pieces together. You can also use the graph paper itself as your template. The benefit of using a paper template is that you can pin your template to the fabric so it won't move when you are tracing the shape onto the fabric. If you are going to use a plastic template, the trick to keeping your fabric stable is to put a piece of sandpaper bumpy side up on your work surface before putting your fabric down. The sandpaper will grip the fabric like Velcro. My teacher Cassandra suggested drawing a design on the outside of an envelope indicating which square pattern is contained therein and storing the pieces accordingly. If you think you're really going to get into the whole quilt-making thing, you could create a binder for all of your quilting projects. You can include each pattern in the binder, along with photographs, fabric swatches, or other things that might be related to that quilt.

The next step in a pieced quilt project is—get this—piecing. And while I explain how to piece something together, I'm going to *simultaneously* give you instructions for making a place mat. You know, kill two birds with one stone.

QUILTING PROJECT NUMBER ONE:

PIECING PRACTICE
PIECED PLACE MATS

Supplies
Plastic template or graph paper template, at least one yard of fabric and four fat quarters, pencil, fabric-cutting scissors, straight pins, sewing needle, standard good-quality cotton thread

Step One: *Templating!* Following the steps above, create two template pieces: your back rectangle piece, which will be 16 inches long by 12 inches wide, and one rectangle that is 8 inches long by 6 inches wide. You will use the small rectangle template repeatedly to make the four rectangle pieces you need for the front of each place mat.

Step Two: *Mark the spot.* Roll your fabric out on a clean tabletop or floor, wrong side up. Choose four different types of fabric that look interesting together. (Bear in mind, you'll need at least a yard of one of the fabrics to create your back pieces.) If the fabric is wrinkled, give it a quick ironing to make it lie smooth and flat. Then lay your first template on the fabric, giving yourself at least a ¼-inch or ½-inch margin on all sides for the seams. Carefully trace your template design onto the fabric using a sharp pencil.

Step Three: *Cut it out!* You're not, I repeat, **not** going to cut exactly along the marked line, though that might seem like the right move. Remember that margin I mentioned for the seams? That's called a seam allowance. You can probably eyeball where you'll need to cut to allow for a ¼-inch seam allowance. But if you want to be precise, you can measure and draw parallel lines ¼ inch outside your template lines before cutting.

Step Four: *Putting it together.* When you've cut all of your pieces (four small rectangles for the front and one big one for the back), you need to get sewing. You want to sew things together in pairs. Grab two of the small pieces and press them together, fancy sides touching. Pin the pieces together at the corners of the lines so the pencil markings line up and then add a few more pins along your seam. If you have drawn your template markings carefully, they will line up perfectly. Then thread your needle (you don't need to double your thread), and tie a double knot at the bottom of it. Remove one of the corner pins, and replace it with the threaded needle. Using a running stitch, sew the pieces together along the drawn line. (The running stitch is made by bringing the needle up through the top of the piece, then back down, then

back up until you are done.) Try
to make the stitches uniform in
length, approximately ¼ inch
long. (Alternately, you can
machine-sew your pieces together.) Sew along the width of
the fabric on one side, and make a
knot when you come to the end.

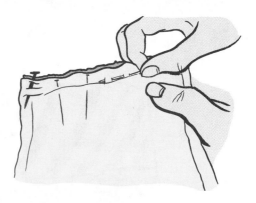

Then sew the next two small
rectangles together. Once you
have two sewn pairs, open
the pairs back up like you are
spreading wings. Take one open
pair and place it flat on the
table, fancy side up. Lay the

second open pair on top of the first pair with the dull side facing up. The fancy sides should be kissing. Pin the pairs together
at the top corners of the rectangle tracing on the fabric. Pick up
your pinned pairs to make sure the pin went through the fabric
precisely on the corner. If it didn't, repin it so that the pin is pierc-
ing the corners of both fabric pairs. Add a few straight pins to

anchor the top edge as well. Now sew along the drawn line. The center seam where the two pieces of fabric join should be flattened
to one side and sewn through. When you are done sewing, you will
have your front piece, which is sewn all together at the cross section.

Step Five: *Completing the task.* To make your place mat more than just a pieced front, you need to put a back on it. Grab the back piece (the one that is 10 inches long by 8 inches wide, plus seam allowance). Now grab the completed front piece and press it against the back piece, fancy sides touching. Pin the back piece and the front piece together at the corners so the pencil markings line up. Sew along three of the four sides, and one-quarter of the way into either end of the fourth side. Snip the corners of the fabric so they won't be bulky when you turn them inside out. Then turn your place mat inside out so that the correct sides are

visible to the world. Use a chopstick or knitting needle to push out your corners. Fold in the open edge of the place mat, and close it using a careful running stitch. Voilà—you have a place mat!

IT'S QUILTING TIME!

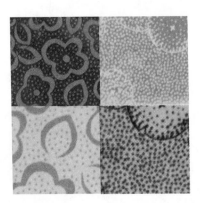

Now I'm going to tell you how basic quilting is done. You can quilt something without having to piece it together first. That's a whole-piece quilt, as I mentioned before. To quilt for warmth, you need to make sure that your stitches are close enough to one another to meet the recommendation on the batting packaging. A closely stitched quilt will have batting that doesn't shift as you sleep. You can get crazy with your designs as long as you follow that minimum-stitching-distance rule. But for the next project, you don't need to follow the minimum-stitching-distance rule—you just want to get that needle through all three layers of fabric.

If you are working on a quilting frame, you are able to do a lot of quilting at once, as long as you have many hands on deck. But for the quilter who dwells in the urban environment or just in a small space, a quilting hoop is the most practical tool for quilting.

QUILTING PROJECT NUMBER TWO:
QUILTED WALL HANGING

Supplies

Plastic template, scissors, hera marker, two squares of fabric approximately 12 inches on each side (one solid color and one patterned), a square of batting 12 inches on each side, quilting hoop, needle, thimble, cotton quilting thread, wide ribbon

Step One: *Template tracing and creating.* Copy the tree design shown onto your template plastic and cut it out. Place the template cutout in the center of your quilt top (which can be either fabric), and trace the outline with a hera marker, which is

a plastic tool that puts a crease in the fabric for you to follow with your stitches.

Step Two: *Hoop dreams.* Layer the fabric and batting together in order of appearance with your hera-marked fabric at the top, then lock the hoop in place. Don't stretch the fabric so it's tight in the hoop as in embroidery—keep it loose for quilting.

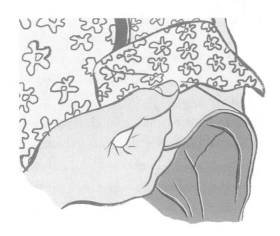

Step Three: *Baste that ~~Turkey~~ quilt.* If you are making a large quilt, you start by basting it. Basting the quilt is essentially binding it together using loose, temporary stitches that run the length and width of the quilt and hold the top, batting, and bottom in place. Really, you baste the whole quilt before you can even get down to quilting. This is yet another reason why I will probably never complete a full quilt. So you know what? Forget step three. Skip ahead to step four. Yeah, that's right, I said skip a step. I give you permission. This is some renegade quilting, my friend—I never said I played by the rules.

Step Four: *A stitch runs through it.* If you were quilting a full quilt, you'd send a running stitch through all three layers of fabric up, down, over, and through the fabric sandwich until you've stitched every last piece at the appropriately spaced intervals.

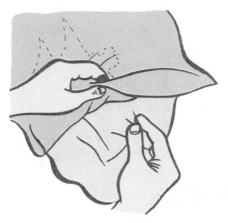

For our small, handquilted wall hanging, you're quilting for the look, not for the warmth. So cut a piece of thread (less than an arm's length), thread your needle, tie a knot at the end, unlock the hoop, and come up for your first stitch between the batting and the top. This will hide your knot. Now re-lock the hoop into place. When you bring the needle back down, you should bring it through all three layers: top, batting, and bottom. Continue to do the running stitch through all three layers, stitching along the outline of the tree. When you are done stitching, unlock the hoop again and hide your closing knot between the batting and the bottom fabric. For super-cuteness and realism, change the color of your thread for the tree trunk.

Step Five: *Trim it!* Pop the layers out of your hoop, and cut down the edges so they are all flush. Pin ribbon along the edges of the square so that half of the ribbon is on the front of the quilt and the other half is folded over onto the back. Using a running stitch, sew into the ribbon from the front side through the three layers and through to the back of the ribbon. Do this along each edge of your square until the wall hanging is completely trimmed. Add two small ribbon loops to the top two corners so you have something to hang the square from. And ta-da—you've got yourself a cool little wall hanging!

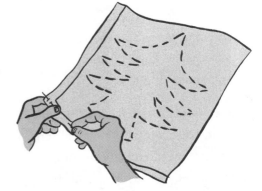

QUILTING PROJECT NUMBER THREE:
QUILTED EARRINGS

Supplies
Fabric scraps, needle, straight pins, scissors, thimble, a few batting scraps, thread (strong cotton or polyester yarn recommended), craft pliers, head pins, fishhook earrings

Optional: *Ruler, graph paper, template plastic*

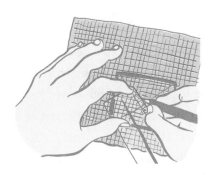

Step One: *Triangulation.* Cut eight triangular pieces of different fabrics, using at least two fabrics for contrast. Triangles should be approximately 1 inch on the short sides and 1½ inches on the long side—whatever size you choose, as long as they are the same. To be precise, you can draw a square on graph paper and divide it into four triangles by drawing two diagonal lines through your square. Trace the triangles onto template plastic, cut them out, and use them to guide your fabric-triangle cutting.

Step Two: *If you think, sew.* Sew triangular pieces together two at a time to form two complete squares made up of four triangles each, mixing and matching the fabrics.

Step Three: *Back in bat.* Cut two pieces of batting and two pieces of backing. Each piece should be approximately 1 ½ inches on each side, making a square.

Step Four: *Build the sandwich and make it stick.* Take your pieced top and layer it on top of the batting and then the back fabric, right side down. Sew with a running stitch through all three

layers in a grid or diagonally across the pieces. That's quilting! When quilted, trim the sides until they are even. Do this with both of your little quilts. They should be the same size when you trim them, give or take ⅛ inch.

Step Five: *All the trimmings.* Cut a strip of fabric 9 inches long and ¾ inch wide. Pin the strip to one edge of the pieced top, folding it so the raw edge isn't visible. Sew a running stitch down the side, stopping ⅛ inch before the end. Create a fold or pucker in

the fabric strip at the corner to allow for the bend. This makes for a soft corner, not a sharp mitered corner. Stabilize it with a few stitches, right at the corner, then continue with the running stitch until you have stitched the strip around all four sides, making a soft fold at each corner.

Turn the square over to the back side. Fold the trim up and under so that the raw edge isn't visible. Then sew a straight running stitch along the edge until it's completely trimmed.

Step Six: *Put the fabric to the metal.* Put a head pin through one of the corners of your tiny quilts. You may need to create a small hole with the tip of a scissors to do so. Using your pliers, create a loop shape with the bottom of the head pin and feed the loop through the bottom loop of the fishhook earring. Close the loop with your pliers. If you don't have a head pin, sew the tiny quilts to the fishhook earrings by sewing through the loop at the fishhook bottom, as shown.

Repeat steps on the second one and, voilà—you've got your sweet earrings!

Quilts make the house warmer, the table brighter, and the ear lovelier. No wonder they're moving back into the crafty spotlight!

CHAPTER NINE

SEPTEMBER

CLAYNATION

One of my favorite things about Crafternoon is talking about it. Talking about Crafternoon almost always leads to one of two things:

1. Finding new Crafternoon converts
2. Getting new Crafternoon ideas

Sometimes it leads to both.

ecently I was talking up Crafternoon with some folks whom I see only on occasion. Somehow, these folks had never heard me mention the 'noon. As you might imagine, they were very excited to hear about it. Turns out that they have a strong love of the craft, and they'd recently had a series of spontaneous crafting sessions that I can only describe as Crafterevenings. After clearing away the dishes at the end of a dinner party, they found themselves breaking out their secret stash of craft supplies. Steve O. has made many awesome puppets in his day, so he has a healthy supply of craft materials lying around the house. We're talking felt, fur, eyes, and thread all just hanging around and waiting to be turned into puppets! When the craft supplies came out, everyone got pumped, and the crafting went on into the wee hours of the morning. They had so much fun doing this the first time, the next time they had folks over for dinner they did the same thing. Their Crafterevenings were becoming a tradition!

As we continued talking, I told them about the Crafternoons I've held in the past and the sorts of crafts we have covered. And then Steve O. asked, "Have you ever held a bust-making Crafternoon?"

I started laughing. "No," I said. "What would that consist of?"

"Everybody would make a bust of someone out of clay," Steve replied.

A bust-making Crafternoon—so strange, so simple, it just might work. Never in a million years would I have thought of hosting a bust-making Crafternoon. Okay, maybe I would have thought of it in a million years, but until cryonics steps up to the plate and extends the shelf life of humans, that's not an option. But Steve O.'s seemingly wild suggestion reminded me of something: The possibilities for Crafternoon are endless. Yup, it's safe to say that Crafternoon is only as limited as your imagination. Sorry if that sounds hokey—it just happens to be true.

To prepare for my bust-making Crafternoon, I remembered back to the bust-making portion of my fifth-grade art class. I'd made a bust of my grandfather, and I felt that it bore a striking resemblance to the man. It was one of my more satisfying art projects. My friend Jeff, who was listening to this craft discussion, also remembered his grammar-school bust making. But his bust efforts were marked by struggle. At his school, you had to bring in a picture of your muse and display it alongside the finished bust. He started his project planning to immortalize a local sports figure, but as the sessions wore on and the clay figure bore no resemblance to the man, he started to panic. Jeff's portrait was so off-kilter that he had to switch photographs at the last minute, choosing another sports figure who bore more resemblance to the final bust. And, according to him, the switch worked. Although the two men looked nothing alike in person, in clay they had switched identities. Let that be a cautionary tale for those embarking on some bust making. You may think you're sculpting your wife's face, but it could turn out to be your mother's. Just make sure you can switch out the picture in time.

So now that I've regaled you with tales of the bust, I'm sure that bust making is the obvious choice for your next Crafternoon. And for those of you who have your doubts, let me say this: You can do more with clay than just get busty. So you shall call this next Crafternoon ClayNation, and the people shall be happy that you did.

There are so many things that one can do with a good lump of clay. For starters, you can reenact the scene from *Ghost* starring Demi Moore and Patrick Swayze. Actually, don't. You need a potter's wheel for that. Our ClayNation Crafternoon will be an extravaganza of doll making and bead rolling, and the kind of clay work that we'll be doing doesn't involve anything more than your hands and a kitchen oven. Oh, and we'll dabble in some bust making, of course—what did I spend the last two pages talking about? Geez, sometimes I think I'm just talking to the air!

GET THE WORD OUT AND SET UP YOUR SPACE

Clay isn't cheap, so you might want to have a good game plan for this 'noon. You can certainly just ask everyone to bring his or her own clay. But if you're concerned that your crafters will show up clayless or, worse, not show up at all, then you can take it upon yourself to purchase the clay supplies. Send your email two weeks before your Crafternoon and tell everyone if they are planning to come, they need to RSVP and they will need to bring X number of dollars for supplies. How do you come up with the X? Here are the minimum amounts of material each crafter will need:

Doll making: *one-quarter of a standard 1.75-pound box of Sculpey per person*

Bust making: *one-half or all of a 1.75-pound box of Sculpey per person*

Bead making: *one 56-gram Fimo block per person*

Go to your local craft store or hit the Internet to find out how much the clay you need costs, and then divide that by the number of people using it. Simple math, folks, simple math. Now you are responsible for going to the craft store or the Internet to purchase the supplies. That means putting up the money and trusting you'll be paid back. In my experience, crafters are a trustworthy bunch. However, there are times when we all experience a tightening of the old purse strings. If this is your circumstance, don't take out a craft-equity loan. And don't put $80 worth of clay on your almost-maxed-out credit card! Do I have to talk to you about interest rates again? Just tell folks to bring their own clay. There may be a few folks who show up clayless, but with any luck, those who came prepared will be willing to share.

It goes without saying that you should feel free to purchase all of the clay yourself and never ask for a penny in return if you're in a position to do so. Look at you, Daddy Warbucks! Money is no object! Buy every color Fimo ever invented! Purchase enough Sculpey to make a life-sized replica of the Great Wall of China! Just make sure you invite me to your party. Speaking of invitations, when I had my clay-tastic Crafternoon, this was the email I sent out to my people:

> Guess what's happening on Sunday from 2 p.m. to 5 p.m.? Well, Crafternoon is happening, silly! And we're going to be making puppets!!! Wow, wow, gee, oh wow, oh wow, oh! Puppets are rad!
>
> We're going to have a guest artist leading us in the craft of puppetry. My friend Lori will be kind enough to show us the way. She is an expert in making beautiful clay puppets! She tells me that if you want to make clay puppets, you should bring Sculpey with you (Super Sculpey if they have it; she says that's the best). Sculpey can be found at art-supply stores and craft centers. Yay, Sculpey! I'll have some Fimo clay on hand for bead making, as well as some water-based acrylic paint and paint-brushes for some other clay-craft projects.
>
> If you are clay-phobic and want to make puppets out of other materials, just bring stuff you think would be fun to work with. Sock puppets are always a blast. I hear that people sometimes lose a sock in the laundry. If that is true, bring the other half of the pair with you, and bring buttons, too! And there is always room to bring your own special crafts.

RSVP, if you see fit. Pass along if you know of missing crafty boys and girls. I do hope to see you.

xoxo,

Maura

Yes, that was the email that I sent when I hosted my clay-based Crafternoon. Lori, the crafter extraordinaire that you may remember as the papermaking teacher and the host of the needlepoint Crafternoon, has been crafting her own clay puppets for a few years now. Her delicate creations look like old china dolls—they have movable arms and legs, gracefully painted faces, and even their own painted-on flapper-girl bobs. During my ClayNation Crafternoon, she showed us how she crafts her puppets, using wire in the arms and legs to give them structure, connecting the limbs but keeping them movable, and painting on their evocative visages. I loved watching the process, but the buck stopped there. There were too many steps to creating the heavenly creatures. I found myself molding a skull for a Day of the Dead altar instead (see the Halloween Crafternoon for project details). But I like the idea of making simple clay dolls, so that's the project you'll find described herein. It's boiled down to the basics, just the way I like it.

While you're playing with your clay, you'll want to have something tasty to share with your crafty companions. Here is a recipe for a spread that highlights the supreme tastiness of one of my all-time favorite veggies—the eggplant. This caponata really makes the eggplant shine, and it's a healthy addition to any Crafternoon.

Blame It on the Caponata

2 tablespoons olive oil
1 medium onion, chopped
2 large cloves garlic, pressed or minced
3 or 4 small eggplants, peeled and cubed
1 red pepper, cored and chopped
¼ pound cremini mushrooms, quartered
One 6-ounce can tomato paste
¼ cup water
2 tablespoons red wine vinegar
¼ cup Morrocan olives, pitted
1 tablespoon fresh oregano, minced
Salt and pepper to taste

Warm the oil in a large pan over medium heat, 1–2 minutes. Add the onions and cook for 2–3 minutes, stirring. Add the garlic and cook for 2 more minutes, stirring.

Once the onions and garlic are soft and aromatic, add the eggplant, pepper, and mushrooms and cook, covered, for 10 minutes, stirring occasionally.

When the eggplant is partially cooked down, add the remaining ingredients and cook, covered, for 30–45 minutes, stirring occasionally. Serve warm or chill overnight and serve with fresh bread. This also makes a yummy pasta sauce!

CLAY PROJECT NUMBER ONE:
CLAY DOLL LIVIN' IN THE CITY

As a kid, I played with dolls like it was going out of
style. Which it was, what with the advent of the
Atari gaming system. Bye, bye, imagination building!
Hello, hand-eye coordination and strategic planning!
But I would not give up my dolls. First, we had no Atari. Second,
playing with dolls allowed me to control everything. I found that
quite enjoyable. I could sit for hours and hours creating endless
storylines and dialogue. The dolls usually played out scenes of
domestic bliss in their dollhouse, but I was willing to abandon
the dollhouse and travel to the Ewok Village if my brother Andy
would play with me. Then the Star Wars action figures would
interact with my perfect suburban family, and Han Solo and Prin-
cess Leia would kiss more than they ever did when George Lucas
was in charge.

For me, the most important thing a doll could do was stand on its
own two feet. Floppy dolls just didn't do it for me. I loved a jointed
doll that could sit *and* stand, but if I had to choose one over the
other, I'd take a standing-only over a sitting-only doll any time. So
I'm going to tell you how to make a clay doll that can stand on its
own two feet.

Supplies
One-quarter of a standard 1.75-pound box of Sculpey clay,
water-based acrylic paint, paintbrushes, an oven

Optional: Wire

Step One: *You get what you knead.* Take a few rows of Sculpey
in your hands and squish it together. Once you've got a serious
clump, start moving it around your hands in a rolling motion, like

you're doing a bad dance move. As the clay becomes more pliable, try rolling it into lines.

Step Two: *The shape of things to come.* When making anything, I find it's easiest to go step by step. You can certainly mold a doll from a single piece of clay, but I prefer to start with a few simple shapes and then combine them together to make the body. Here are the shapes that make a body:

Small round ball (*a.k.a. the head*)

Short log (*a.k.a. the neck*)

Large triangular piece (*a.k.a. the torso*)

Four longer logs (*a.k.a. two arms and two legs*)

Two more short logs (*a.k.a. the feet*)

That's the basic body format. If you're planning to add other body accoutrements (potbellies, tails, ample bosoms, horns, etc.), reserve some clay for those additions.

Step Three: *Assembly line.* Now assemble the body in order: head, neck, torso, legs, and arms. (You should know what goes where—I'm not going to help you with that.) I prefer to put things together on a flat surface initially, then get my guy standing upright. Your doll should stand upright once it is fired as long as the feet are flat and it's not too top-heavy.

Step Four: *Make no mistake.* One of the really great things about clay is that you can swiftly and thoroughly erase any errors. All you need is your thumb and a little precision and, voilà—the crease separating the arm from the torso just disappears. This is not an option with crafts involving painting, gluing, cutting, taping, sawing, nailing, puffy-painting, glass blowing, surgery, or Ouija boards. And while you can undo what you've done in knitting, knotting, and sewing, it's usually a laborious task. In the world of clay, it's smooth sailing.

If you're dissatisfied with your clay creation at any point before you fire it, you can modify individual elements, or you can pound the whole thing back into a lump and start all over again. It's pretty fun to pound clay, so I understand if you feel compelled to do so. But to make slight modifications, use your fingers to mold or remold your problem spots. If something isn't looking the way you want it to, try again. For more difficult-to-reach areas, take a piece of metal wire (the Sculpey box recommends armature wire) and fold it over once so it forms a U-shaped loop. This loop makes for a great scraping tool. You can keep making ch-ch-changes until you get bored, and the clay will stay supple. Until you bake it, that is. Once your clay is baked, you can forget about changing it. It will be solid as a rock—just like our love of crafting.

Step Five: *Shake and bake.* Follow directions! The box tells us some important things about working with this material: Bake at 130°F for 15 minutes per ¼ inch of thickness. If you've got something that has various degrees of thickness, I'd undercook it before I'd overcook it, given the fact that the box says, "DO NOT exceed the above temperature or recommended baking time." Those are their all caps, not mine. Always read the manufacturer's instructions! Check your box of clay before even opening it—you want to be prepared, just like a Boy Scout. And don't plan to eat, drink, or smoke out of your doll. This stuff is strictly decorative, baby.

Step Six: *Give it a fresh coat of paint.* While you can certainly leave your dolly naked as the day she was fired, it's fun to paint on some personality. After you've fired the doll and let it cool, give your doll some hair, some clothes, and maybe even a face, using your trusty paintbrushes and acrylic paint. And then when you've gotten her to look just like you want her to, put the brushes down, let her dry, and say hello, dolly!

CRAFTY INTERLUDE:
Good *for You!*

When one is crafting, it's easy to get lost in the process of it. I find that I have no trouble knitting away hours and hours, completely engaged in the process. Crafting encourages my mind to focus—it becomes something akin to meditation. And because of the way that it shifts the mind's focus, crafting provides sweet relief from worries. My friend Betty was telling me that Winston Churchill took up oil painting because it was so engrossing that it took his mind off everything else. And I think that Winston had a lot on his mind. Now, some folks may say that knitting and oil painting aren't the same thing, and they're right. Just try to wear an oil painting on a brisk October day. But oil painting and knitting both provide the same old-fashioned escapism, and a little escapism never hurt anyone. In fact, a little escapism can be a big help to a lot of people, especially when you can escape within a productive environment. Just ask your doctor. He or she will tell you that Crafternoon is good for your health.

Now, some folks may take issue with this argument. "So, you say that crafting is good for your health, eh? Maybe you've never tried following the pattern for a cable-knit sweater with a cowl neck! That gave me a migraine and ten unused skeins of yarn! And hey, where were you when I was trying to get my crazy quilt to act a little more normal? That was no good for my blood pressure. Why don't you try to do some hard crafts and then let's talk!"

To those folks I say, "Geez, why the hostility? I never said crafting was *always* relaxing. But it is usually engrossing. When you're trying to figure out where you dropped a stitch, I know it can be really frustrating, but chances are, in that frustrating moment, you are still completely focused on the task at hand. And that focus is satisfying all on its own."

I admit that I'm not much for difficult patterns and complicated crafts, so I'm less likely to have a lot of frustrating moments. And I like that. If I'm following my own pattern and I can't figure out how to get past a difficult step, sometimes I'll find another way to approach it. Or sometimes I'll set it aside until I'm ready to come back and give it my full attention. Everyone is an individual. What is relaxing for me might be frustrating for you. What gives my mind focus might send yours scattering in a million different directions. So do what's best for you, and craft the way you want to. That's the whole point of Crafternoon. We all do something on our own, with the support and comfort of each other. So I'm not saying that crafting is easy; I'm just saying that it's good for you.

CLAY PROJECT NUMBER TWO:

YOU'RE A HEART BREAKER, BEAD MAKER

Supplies
Three different-colored 56-gram Fimo blocks, Kabob stick or chopstick, baking sheets, an oven

You've already discovered how totally awesome clay can be. You've used it to make a doll. You're about to learn how to use it to make a bust. But first, use it to make some wearable craft. There are a million ways to make a bead, but I like the one that's simplest. Sure, you could create beads that have precise patterns and shapes, but you'll have to look on the Internet for those instructions. I'm not that into precision. I like to make a bead that's got the hippie-dippy vibe written all over it. So here are some simple instructions for a little bead I like to call the Smushie.

Step One: *Choose your colors.* Choose three or more colors of Fimo clay to work with. Take a small, fingertip-sized pinch of clay in each color.

Step Two: *Smush it!* Put the pinches together in the palm of your hand, and roll them around until they form a ball. This should create a swirling, multicolored bead design. If the ball is larger than you wanted, you could pinch it in half and reroll it into two smaller beads. You can also play with the shape of the beads by rolling them in your hands: For a more circular bead, roll the ball around in your hand completely. For an oval bead, roll the bead back and forth from the center so that the edges of the bead will pop slightly. To make squares, press your bead into a tabletop and flatten it on each side using a ruler, CD case, or any other straight surface.

Step Three: *Poke it!* Using a kabob stick (available in most grocery stores) or a chopstick, poke a hole through the center of each of your beads. The end of the bead may look sloppy where the hole was made. You can delicately fix this with either the tip of the stick or the pad of your finger. Gently hold the bead while you make any changes—you don't want to squish it further at this stage.

Step Four: *Bake it!* Bake your beads on a clean baking sheet in a 230°F oven for 30 minutes. When the beads are done, they will be hard and ready to string on your next masterpiece necklace or on your Bo Derek braids.

CLAY PROJECT NUMBER THREE:
BUSTED!

Making a bust is as simple as can be. All you need is some clay and a muse. If you're not sure whom to immortalize in your new bust, take a gander at your holiday gift list. When you find the person who has everything, that's your bust recipient. Because even the person who has everything probably does not have a bust of himself or herself, but the person who has everything definitely wants one.

Supplies
One-half of a 1.75-pound box of Sculpey or Super Sculpey, craft wire, an oven

Optional: Water-based acrylic paint, paintbrushes

Step One: *Get in shape!* Make an oval-shaped ball with half of your portion of clay. Reserve half of the remaining clay to make a neck and shoulders and the other half for add-on features.

Step Two: *It's all in the details.* Using your reserved clay, add a nose, mouth, eyes, and eyebrows to the head. Use craft wire to carve additional details, like wrinkles, into the face. On the other hand, if you are giving this as a gift, you might want to forgo the wrinkles.

Step Three: *Get your head on straight.* Form the neck by rolling a big log out of your remaining clay, then spreading the clay out along the bottom of it with your thumbs to form the shoulders. Attach your head to your neck by carefully pressing the two parts together. Using a wire loop or just your fingers, blend the clay from the head and the neck together.

Step Four: *Bakeshop!* Follow the instructions on your Sculpey box to bake your bust at the right temperature for solid goodness through and through. Paint after baking, if desired.

No matter what you want, you'll get what you knead out of a ClayNation Crafternoon. Even if you spend the afternoon just squishing a ball of clay in your hand, you'll be making good use of your time. Consider it physical therapy, minus the massive rubber bands and plus your friends.

CHAPTER TEN

OCTOBER

COSTUME-MAKING CAVALCADE AND HOMESPUN-ATTIRE EXTRAVAGANZA

When October approaches, I immediately begin thinking about the best holiday of the year—Halloween! Man, for an intrinsically puritan nation, we definitely embrace the pagan good times that Halloween provides. I love Halloween! It's the biggest and most original party of the year. And who can resist dressing up, 'cause how often do you get to roam the streets incognito? I get my Halloween thinking cap on early, and as you might imagine, I like to add an element of handicraft whenever possible. Just as I've started really thinking hard about the 'ween, the stores start to fill up with mass-produced costumes. Kids and adults alike are targeted to purchase these thousands-of-a-kind, disposable garments. Whether you're in the market to dress up like Superman or a French maid, I can tell you there's a prêt-à-porter, one-size-fits-all costume hanging in a bag at your local chain pharmacy or pop-up Halloween superstore.

Who else is creeped out by these stores? Is it just me, or is it weird to go to a store that's open for only six weeks a year? Halloween superstores and tax-preparation centers are the only businesses that annually occupy a storefront for a brief blip on the year's calendar. Mass-produced costumes sales and tax-preparation services are two things I just can't get psyched about. Due to either an aversion to the ghosts of tax seasons past or my natural desire to stand out in a crowd, I have never purchased a costume from a store. Wait—I did buy one once. I bought an ALF costume from a store in Bay Ridge in Brooklyn a few years ago.

(This was a solid 15 years after the peak of ALF's popularity, and the costume had the dust to prove it.) I was intending to keep the ALF mask around until I had children and could try to explain the bizarre television trend of alien-out-of-water stories, but a friend ended up borrowing it to wear one Halloween, and I never got it back. Farewell, sweet ALF. I hope I'll find you again someday.

I'm not saying that every homemade Halloween costume I've ever worn has been a hit. I've certainly had my share of misses, starting in third grade, the first year that we made our own Halloween costumes in art class. That year I was a penguin, and my machine-sewn black-and-white costume was close to perfect, with one exception. I forgot to make a beak. So rather than looking like a bird, I looked like a Mummenschanz mime. And that was not cool. But I learned a valuable lesson that year—when you're choosing a Halloween costume, the difference between a hit and a miss is all in the details.

I'd like to tell you that that was the last time that I had a bad costume, but third grade was a while ago. My most recent bad costume was Halloween 2004, when I dressed up as Billy Joel and Rufus dressed up as Elton John. The concept was this: Piano Men of the '70s. Now, if properly executed, this costume could have been really great. Unfortunately, I completely failed in my preparatory work. I know, I said I always start thinking about Halloween really early in the season, and that year was no exception. The problem was not in the thinking; it was in the not doing. Yes, I thought about the costume a lot, but somehow I managed to leave all of the doing until the last minute, the weekend of all the big Halloween parties. I hit the stores to get a black curly wig, and I couldn't find a thing. I know, I said I don't buy costumes in stores, but a wig is not a whole costume—it's an element in a larger costume. I like wigs, and I have yet to learn how to make my own wig. I think that stores can be useful for certain things—things that help enhance a homemade or home-devised costume. As Billy Joel once sang, "I'm only human." Sing it, Billy. Sing it.

So, I already had a big, boxy blazer and I'd created a five o'clock shadow effect by dotting my face with eyeliner. But a boxy blazer and a five o'clock shadow do not a Billy Joel make. What they do make is a hobo. Ninety percent of those surveyed thought I was rocking the hobo look. I can bet that most of them wondered where I had left my bandana-sack-on-a-stick. They had no clue I was going for Joel. And Rufus? Well, they just thought he was a sleazy disco dude. They had no idea that he was the beloved Honky Cat.

Those two tales are not meant to dissuade you from making your own clever Halloween getup. On the contrary, I'm just reminding you that even those of us who are sworn to a life of original Halloween costumes sometimes fail in our attempts. But look at me, preaching to the converted! Crafty folks are always the folks most likely to make their own costumes, and I'm sure you're no different. So let's get started on our costume-making cavalcade!

GET THE WORD OUT AND SET UP YOUR SPACE

It's not hard to get people stoked about Halloween, but you still want your email to be fun and enticing. Here's what I penned to get the crafters crawling out of their creaky castles:

> Come to a Creepy Crafternoon at High Noon! Oh, my crafty ghouls and boys, Halloween is nearly upon us. Are you ready for the big night? Wouldn't you like to be ready? Then please, won't you join me this Sunday for a creepy Crafternoon?
>
> The theme, of course, is Halloween. Bring your costumes and work on them in the company of friends. But there will be other projects to capture your crafty imagination, too, such as Day of the Dead skulls. If you prefer to do your own thing, you can be sure your personal craft projects are always welcome.
>
> If you'd like to bring some eating or drinking items, please do! All eats are appreciated. If you'd like to bring crafting materials to share, I think that's grand! I hope to see you there!
>
> xoxo,
>
> Maura

TREAT OF THE 'NOON:
Frighteningly Good Pumpkin-Carrot-Walnut Bread

Come October 1, I begin to get a strong craving for all things pumpkin. There's something about that sweet winter squash that makes my heart sing and my mouth water. Autumn is my absolute favorite time of the year, and nothing says autumn like a pumpkin. My mom's been making pumpkin bread for as long as I can remember, and I always loved it. When I moved to California in 1997, someone passed along to me a new pumpkin bread recipe, and I found that it was quite different from my mom's pumpkiny style. Recently I adapted my California recipe to feature a new twist: the carrot. And the results are quite tasty indeed. Here is a new autumn favorite.

1 ¾ cups white whole-wheat flour
1 ⅓ cups sugar
1 teaspoon baking soda
1 teaspoon ground cinnamon
½ teaspoon salt (use ¼ teaspoon if using salted butter)
½ teaspoon ground nutmeg
⅛ teaspoon allspice

⅛ teaspoon ground cloves
1 cup canned pumpkin puree
1 egg, beaten
⅓ cup water
½ cup butter, melted
½ cup grated carrots
¼ cup chopped walnuts (optional)

Preheat the oven to 350°F. In a large bowl, sift together the flour, sugar, baking soda, cinnamon, salt, nutmeg, allspice, and cloves. In another bowl, mix the pumpkin, egg, water, and butter until smooth. Add the wet ingredients to the dry ingredients gradually, mixing completely but just until moistened. Then add the carrots and walnuts and mix.

Grease and flour three or four mini loaf pans. Fill each with batter. Bake for 45 minutes, or until a toothpick inserted into the center comes out clear. Slide a knife around the sides of each pan, then turn them out onto cooling racks. Allow them to partially cool before cutting. Serve when warm for maximum deliciousness.

HALLOWEEN PROJECT NUMBER ONE:
PAPIER-MÂCHÉ MASKS

Mask making is one of the most fun things you can possibly do, ever. One year Rufus suggested that we make masks to wear to our friend Lecy's Halloween cocktail party, so the night before the big event, we had our friend George over for dinner and started on the mask project. This project involves papier-mâché, and papier-mâché is a highly messy two-step process, with a drying period of 24 hours in between.

Since the papier-mâché takes a whole day to dry, you would need to prep for your Crafternoon in advance by making enough papier-mâché bases for everyone to work with. For our base, we used balloons and tried to make sure that they were blown up to a size slightly wider than our faces. (If you're the kind of person who's already got a plaster cast of your own face lying around the house, then now is the perfect time to break it out for your mask base. It would be pretty cool to make a mask that fits your face like a glove.)

Supplies
Newspaper, one cup flour, three cups water, balloons, a big basin, paints, paintbrushes, X-Acto blade, elastic

Optional: *Aluminum foil*

Step One: *Clear the table.* Prepare your workspace by covering it with some newspaper or a plastic tablecloth.

Step Two: *Mix it!* In your basin, mix one cup flour with three cups water, stirring thoroughly to make a slippery paste.

Step Three: *Mush it!* Tear newspaper into strips 1 to 2 inches wide. Dump clumps of strips into the basin, mushing the mixture around with your hands. Keep stuffing as many strips into the basin as you can fit, mixing completely.

Step Four: *Balloon art.* Blow up your balloon as big as possible. Hold it up to your head—it needs to be slightly bigger than your head, or the mask will be too small. Then begin covering the front of the balloon with strips of wet newspaper in crisscross patterns. If you feel so inclined, make a ring out of aluminum foil and stabilize your balloon by placing it in the aluminum ring. Keep adding strips until the "face" surface is completely covered. You can smooth out the surface with your fingertips when you are done adding all the strips. Add several layers of strips so your mask will be sturdy and in it to win it.

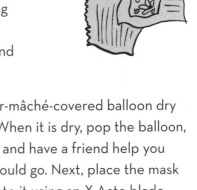

Step Five: *Decorate.* Let the papier-mâché-covered balloon dry for a whole day before painting it. When it is dry, pop the balloon, then hold the mask up to your face and have a friend help you mark where the eyes and mouth should go. Next, place the mask on a table and carefully cut holes into it using an X-Acto blade. When you've got your holes in the right place, you can paint on any design your crafty heart desires.

Step Six: *Fasten it.* Using the pointy end of a pair of scissors, poke one small hole into each side of the mask near ear level. Make a knot in one end of your elastic, and feed it into one hole. Measure out how much elastic you will need to secure the mask around your head. Cut the elastic, then knot it on the outside. Ta-da—you have a mask!

HALLOWEEN PROJECT NUMBER TWO: I'M BEGINNING TO SEE A PATTERN

Okay, future sexy witch, you know exactly how you want your costume to look, but you haven't got a clue how to make it. You could try to use your magic wand to make one appear, but the glitter you glued to it is still drying. Looks like you're going to have to whip up that costume yourself with your very own magic hands. But you can do it—I think you've got the Gift.

To get the ball rolling on a handmade costume, most folks would go to the nearest fabric store, flip through their big books of patterns, choose one, and then follow the directions. And if you're feeling the fever, that's exactly what you should do. But I'm not like most folks, and I'm a little intimidated by patterns. All those crazy lines and arrows drawn every which way make me feel sort of crazy. And I can never really figure out what the thing is going to look like once it's chopped and sewn and covering my body. So I prefer a more primitive pattern-making system, one I like to call "Sew with What You Know."

Supplies
Kraft paper (butcher paper), straight pins, pencil, fabric, fabric scissors, sewing machine or hand needle and thread plus patience!

Step One: *Your next top model.* Start by reaching into your closet. Pull out your favorite simple dress or skirt or pair of pants, the one whose basic shape most closely mimics the design you're looking to replicate. If it's got gussets and pleats and smocking and lace inlay, put it back right now. First of all, didn't anyone ever tell you that dress has too much going on? It's as busy as the subway at rush hour! And secondly, there is no way you're going to figure out how to replicate that using your own pattern. Unless you went to Fashion Institute of Technology. If you did, please skip over this section. I can tell you right now, you will find my garment-making methodology completely deplorable.

Step Two: *Prepare the canvas.* So you've chosen your garment to clone. Now you need to turn it into a pattern you can copy. For this, a roll of kraft paper will be your best friend forever. You can try to buy a roll at your local shipping-supply store or order a roll online. Give your floor a clean sweep, then roll out your kraft paper. (Even though kraft-paper projects tend to take up a lot of space when the paper's rolled out, it's nice to have a small roll of it around for pattern making, wrapping paper creating, and impromptu mural parties.) So, you've got your paper on the floor. Now turn your chosen garment inside out and lay it flat on the paper. Lay the arms outstretched. Smooth out any wrinkles, then, using a few pins, anchor the garment to the kraft paper at some key spots.

Step Three: *Trace it up!* Next, carefully trace the outline of the garment with a pencil. When you have completed your tracing, remove the garment and hang it back up in the closet. Don't just leave it there on the floor, collecting dust. I thought you said it was your favorite? I'm not going to get you anything new if that's how you're going to treat your things.

So you've got your paper tracing. But the outline you made is not the final pattern. Remember, your garment has seams in it. Yup, seams! From the waist of the garment outline, measure ⅝-inch out, then mark that point on your paper. Now, using a ruler, draw a line parallel to the garment ⅝ inch away from the outline. For the

hem (that's at the bottom of your garment, for those who are hem-ignorant), give yourself 2 inches extra. For rounded areas, use a compass (the one you used to use in geometry class, not the one you used that one time you went camping) to add your ⅝-inch seam line in a precise and geometric fashion. Once you've created the seam line, cut along the outside line and pop that pattern out!

Step Four: *Fabric finding.* Fabric is a necessary component of most garment making. You can try using aluminum foil or your hopes and dreams, but it is traditional to make garments out of fabric. So now that you've got yourself a pattern, you need to take yourself to the store to buy some fabric. But before you run out the door, you need to get the measurements of the garment. Simply measure the height and the width of your pattern at the highest and the widest points and double it. That accounts for the front *and* the back of the garment. When you get to the fabric store, you're going to be asked to make your purchase in yard form. One yard = three feet. So, you do the math. Remember, you want to give yourself enough room to have some space around your pattern. And there is nothing wrong with ending up with remnants. Remember the quilting chapter? The extra fabric will be the raw material for your next quilting project.

I recommend that you purchase the cheapest fabric to suit your needs. You're making a costume, which means you won't be wearing it every day. That is, unless you *are* going to wear it every day. In that case, you should buy the best fabric possible, but maybe save some cash for a few therapy sessions. Either way, as a newbie seamster/

seamstress, you might not nail your patterns the first time around. Buying cheaper fabric allows you some emotional wiggle room if something goes wrong.

Step Five: *Pin and cut!* Start by ironing your newly purchased fabric, then pin your pattern to it. To save time, you should work with the fabric doubled over so that you cut both sides of your garment at the same time. Following your pattern, take your time as you cut out that sweet shape!

Step Six: *Sewing the seeds of Halloween love.* Pin your pieces with the fancy/design sides together so the dull side of the fabric is facing out. Place a pin perpendicular to your edge every 2 to 3 inches to maximize the stability of your sewing. Then sew that puppy closed! If you're using a sewing machine, it should have a setting for a ⅝-inch seam allowance. If you are handsewing, just mark ⅝-inch in from the edge of your fabric approximately every 6 inches so that you will stay on mark with your seam. If your garment is a tight-fitting number, copy the opening on the original and create an opening on your own. Add snaps, which are easily hand sewn, so that it closes. If you don't leave an opening, you'll have a tough time getting into your garment, unless someone is going to sew you into it. At the bottom of the garment, you can fold up the fabric and sew a 2-inch hem to give your garment a finished edge, or you can just cut carefully along the edge to even it out. You're not going to wear this for more than a night or two, so it doesn't need to be perfectly finished. Now turn your garment right side out and wear your handiwork!

CRAFTY INTERLUDE:
A Simpler Way to Unique Costumes

Some of the best costumes can be created by modifying an existing garment. A few years back, I was invited to a costume party at a Russian bath. This party was a dream come true for me because it involved bathing, which I love, and costumes, which I lurve. I wanted to take the classy route on the bathing costume, so I was trying to figure out how to craft an old-fashioned bathing suit. I wanted to look like a Depression-era bather, minus the depression. I was really busy, so I drew some patterns and decided to try to convince my mother to whip up something for me. But as the party drew closer and I hadn't managed to get my butt over to my parents' house to ask for costuming assistance, it began to look more and more as though my costume was going to consist of a modern bathing suit and a wig, which seemed odd. And then, like a flash of lightning, the inspiration hit. Somewhere in my closet lived a 1970s jumpsuit that I had bought at a thrift store many years before. I couldn't remember ever having worn it outdoors since it was skintight. (It was a sleeveless number that flared out into bell-bottoms when it hit the floor.) I realized that by chopping off the legs, I would have a bathing costume. And that is exactly what I did. Off went the legs, and in came a simple hem I sewed by hand. For the party, I tied a silk scarf around my head and donned some big sunglasses to give me that old-time movie-star glamour, and I was off and bathing. From that night on, that bathing costume has become one of my favorite bathing suits ever.

HALLOWEEN PROJECT NUMBER THREE:
CELEBRATION SKULL

Supplies

Sculpey clay, an oven, black and white water-based acrylic paint, paintbrush

Optional: *Several colors of tissue paper, construction paper, scissors, glue*

Día de los Muertos, which translates to "Day of the Dead," is a Mexican celebration of our dearly departed. This holiday encourages us to remember those who have passed before us, with joy, rather than sorrow. Altars are made to honor loved ones with their favorite food and drink, as well as flowers and candles and skulls and skeletons. The Day of the Dead treats death as a natural part of the cycle of life, not something to live in fear of, and treats our departed loved ones as spirits who maintain a presence in our lives. And I happen to think that is something worth crafting for.

Step One: *Work it.* Grab a handful of Sculpey clay and roll it around in your palms to form a smooth ball.

Step Two: *Mold it.* To form the shape of a skull, lay your clay ball flat on a table or other smooth surface. Pull out the lower front part of the clay to create the jaw. Round the top and back of the head so it looks like a skull (give it a ridge in the back to give it more authenticity). Now gently press your thumbs into the clay on either side of the face to make eye sockets. Using your pointer finger, make a smaller indentation for the nose. Don't bother making a mouth yet; you'll paint one on later. When you feel that your clay ball looks sufficiently skull-like, stop playing with it.

Step Three: *Bake it.* Following the instructions on your box of clay, bake your skull in the oven. Let it cool before painting.

Step Four: *Paint it.* Paint the whole skull white. When it's completely dry, paint the eye and nose sockets black. Draw a black line across the mouth area and crisscross it with lines to create the appearance of teeth. You can add swirls or other decorative embellishments around the top and back of the skull if you like, or leave it plain and simple.

Step Five: *Dress it up (optional).* To make your skull more festive, place it on a bed of tissue-paper flowers. Cut two strips of tissue paper approximately 6 inches long and 1 inch wide. Fold each strip in an accordion pattern. Pinch the strips on one side and hold them together. Then wrap the pinched sides with a pipe cleaner or twist-tie to secure the strips to each other. Then fan the strips out on the open sides so they look like a flower. Place your skull in the center. Voilà—you have a lovely addition to your altar!

Just remember: Halloween isn't just for kids; it's for crafters of all ages. So get out there and craft yourself a one-of-a-kind costume to celebrate one-of-a-kind you!

appliqué hearts where the word heart should be. I thought the shirts were hilarious because they were so presumptuous, and it's weird to see someone sell handmade T-shirts at a comedy show. But the shirts completely sold out. Maybe it was because I only had time to make four of them.

The novelty of the puffy paint wore off around the same time that I decided to move back to New York. My then boyfriend Peter was also moving to the East Coast, to Providence, Rhode Island, so we decided to make the cross-country journey together, as I mentioned way back in the introduction. I had my learner's permit and was hoping to get some driving in, but I knew there would be lots of long stretches where Peter would be doing all of the driving. I needed to do something with my hands while I sat and looked out the window. So while I was in New York preparing my way back home before flying back to SF to gather my things and embark upon the big drive, I enlisted my mother to teach me how to knit. She got me started on my knitting way. And while it took me lots of rows of terrible, sloppy stitching, I did eventually get the hang of the knitting. Then she tried to teach me to purl but I refused, saying I wanted to get knitting down before I branched out into the intimidating world of purling. She thought I was acting crazy, but she just sighed and shook it off. I'm stubborn as all hell when I want to be.

My first-ever knit project was a cross-country scarf. I figured that since Peter was slated to do most of the driving on our trip, he deserved a beautiful knit thing as a souvenir from our big trip. And he ended up doing *all* of the driving, so he most definitely deserved it. I chose yellow and green yarn, the colors of the Oakland A's, his favorite baseball team. And then all across America, while he drove, I knit. I knit in California, Arizona, New Mexico, Texas, Arkansas, Mississippi, Alabama, Georgia, South Carolina, North Carolina, Virginia, the District of Columbia, Maryland,

Delaware, New Jersey, and finally New York. I knit in the deserts, I knit in the forests, I knit on the wide, open plains. Somewhere in Arkansas I picked up a skein of multicolored yarn and threw that into the knit mix. It felt great to be moving back home, and it felt great to knit a testament to the journey. And I was grateful to Peter for taking me on such an awesome adventure, so the least I could do was knit him a scarf.

After I completed Peter's scarf, I immediately moved on to my next scarf. I knit scarves for my parents, my friends, myself—basically anyone who had a neck that needed warming. I experimented with different yarns—organic, hand-dyed woolen yarn, yarn made from old kimonos, yarn with fuzzy edges that knit up to look like a feather boa, yarn of every shape and size. And when Peter and I stopped dating, I knitted up a storm. It distracted me from my sadness by keeping me looking to the next stitch, the next complete row, and the next good thing. And when I was finally ready, I asked my mom to help me move on, and she did. She taught me how to purl.

My first real purling project was a baby hat for a friend's sister. I still wasn't all that excited about purling or pattern reading, but I knew it had to be done. See, scarves make great gifts for just about everybody, except for babies and small children. Scarves are a *terrible* gift for babies and small children. Hats, on the other hand, make a fantastic gift for babyhood to small child-hood. So for the sake of the babies, I purled *and* read patterns.

So, that's the history of knitting and me in a nutshell. Like so many other knitters out there, I love its therapeutic quality. You get into a rhythm and forget there is anything else in the world. It also gives me a swift sense of accomplishment. In our attention-deficient, multitasking culture, relaxation and concrete accom-plishments are often hard to come by. I can multitask with the best of them, but I don't like it. I'd rather sit for a moment and knit myself into a meditative state. It's much better for the blood pressure.

GET THE WORD OUT AND SET UP YOUR SPACE

Here's the invitation I sent out to my crafters to get them amped to rock the needles:

Join me this Saturday for an afternoon of getting your knit on. We'll teach and we'll learn some knitting, purling, garter stitching, and so on. Those of us who can already knit will do some showing off/mentoring, but we'll also have the opportunity to ask my mom more advanced questions about reading patterns, completing garments, etc. Just don't ask my mom about circular needles. My mom is not down with circular needles.

For those of you who are without supplies, you can join us at 2 p.m. at my favorite knitting store in Brooklyn to make some purchases. The store's got all different types of yarn including acrylics, which are cheap and good for beginners. And a set of needles will set you back between $5 and $10. I'm guessing we'll mill around for half an hour looking at the goods and advising newbies on what to purchase. Then we'll walk back to my house and get knitty with it!

Treats of the edible or potable varieties are welcomed and encouraged. Hope to see you there!

xoxo,

Maura

TREAT OF THE 'NOON:
Psyche-delicata Squash and Parsnipy Soup

My friend Miriam is a farmer in upstate New York. She delivers food to Brooklyn once a week during the growing season to lucky folks like me who are part of her farm-share program. Farm-share or community-supported agriculture (CSA) programs invite members to pay small farms a membership fee before the growing season that is then used to help cover the expenses of the farm. In return, members receive bounties of exceedingly delicious and totally nutritious food on a weekly or biweekly basis from growers they actually know and at a better price, too. Joining Miriam's farm share is one of the best things I did this year. I highly recommend farm shares to anyone who likes eating. Do some research and find out if there is a farm-share program near you.

Okay, so, all of that info was me setting the stage for this delicious soup. In one of my shares, I received some delicious delicata squash. This squash is more delicate than butternut squash, hence the name. And it has a lovely flavor. We also got loads of leeks, so I figured I'd make a great soup with the squash and the leeks, and I threw in some parsnips to give it a little attitude. I like a little attitude in my food.

2 medium delicata squashes (about 2 pounds)
3 medium parsnips, cored and quartered
4 tablespoons olive oil
2 large leeks, white parts only, chopped
2 cups chicken or vegetable stock
½ cup water
3 fresh rosemary leaves, torn
½ teaspoon honey

Preheat the oven to 350°F. Cut the squash lengthwise and remove all of the seeds and stringy parts. Place them on a baking sheet scooped side down, and bake for approximately 45 minutes.

Coat the parsnips in 2 tablespoons of oil and place them in a baking dish or pan. Add the pan to the oven when the squash has 25 minutes of baking time remaining. The parsnips should be slightly browned when done.

After removing the squash from the oven, allow them to cool down enough for you to handle. Then scrape the flesh of the squash from the skin. This process is kind of annoying and laborious, but just take your time and Zen out. It's totally worth it. Squash is so yummy and filling—just keep that in mind as you try to wrangle your hot squash.

In a large pot, warm 2 tablespoons of oil over medium heat, and add the leeks. Cook until soft, then add the stock, squash, water, and rosemary. Smush and stir the squash in the mixture for 5–10 minutes, until mixed and aromatic.

Transfer the squash-leek-liquid combo to a heatproof food processor. Add the parsnips and honey, and puree until you reach the desired consistency. For a thinner soup, you can add a little more water and puree for longer. Serve with fresh bread and enjoy!

GET RIGHT DOWN TO THE REAL KNITTY-GRITTY: A PRACTICAL APPROACH

First things first: Patience is a virtue, especially when it comes to tackling a new craft. So, while you first-time knitters will want to catch up to the knitty-est kids on the block, remember this: Knitting is harder than it looks, but it's easier than you think.

Choose the right needle to go with your chosen yarn. First-time knitters can start with a simple four-ply yarn and pair it with size 7 or 8 needles. A smooth, simple cotton, acrylic or washable wool yarn in a light color is your best choice. So go get your yarn and your needles and let's get started!

Knitting consists of three things:

1. Casting on

2. Knitting

3. Casting off

If you are going to purl, you can throw that into the mix wherever your desire or wherever your pattern directs you to. So let's go step-by-step through the process and then tackle some cool knitting projects!

CASTING ON
(a.k.a. *Throwing Loops on a Stick*)

Step One: *Loop-de-loop.* Make a basic knot loop. To do this, grasp about 6 inches of the yarn, holding it taut between both hands and anchoring it between your thumb and pointer finger in each hand. Give yourself an extra 6 inches of yarn on the loose side of the yarn—you'll sew that into your piece when you're done. Walk your submissive hand over to your dominant hand so your fingers kiss. Your yarn should form a loop above your hands. Grasp the bottom of the loop (the place where the yarn overlaps) with your dominant hand. Grasp the tail of yarn on the submissive side and lift it up, behind and through the open loop. Keep the loop open.

Step Two: *Poke it!* Hold one of your two needles in your dominant hand with the open end of the needle facing away from you. Poke the needle through the loop you created, then pull the knot tight on the needle.

The arch of the knot should be on the top of the needle, with the bumpy knot part on the bottom. That's your first stitch!

Step Three: *Keep On Casting On!* Leave the tail dangling at the end of your needle. Now take hold of the next section of yarn in your submissive hand and hold it taut behind your outstretched thumb and pointer finger. Your palm should be facing toward you. Walk your submissive hand over to your dominant hand, making the yarn form another simple loop. Pull this loop onto the

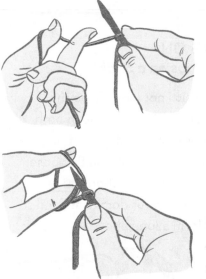

needle and tighten it. You've just completed your second stitch! Repeat this motion until you have the correct number of stitches to follow your chosen pattern. You'll get into a rhythm with it (it's pretty rockin' once you get going). If you lose track of the number of stitches, just count the number of lines on the top of your needle. If you are just looking to do some practice knitting, cast on 10–15 stitches to start.

KNIT!
(a.k.a. How to Make a Knot Using a Needle)

Step One: *Brace yourself.* With your bare needle in your dominant hand and your stitch-heavy needle in your submissive one, hold both needles with the pointy ends facing out. Hold the bare needle akin to the way you hold a pencil, but position your pointer finger higher up along the end of the needle. The thumb of your submissive hand should be positioned at the front open end of the needle it's holding, with all the other fingers at the back acting as a brace.

Step Two: *Enter the ~~dragon~~ stitch.* Enter the first stitch (the one at the open end of the needle) with the tip of the bare needle at an angle from below so that the needle comes out behind the stitch-heavy needle, with the tip of the needle pointing in the direction of your submissive hand. The needles should form an X.

Step Three: *Grasp it!* Without letting go of the stitchy needle, grasp the tip of the bare needle with your submissive hand. Now you've got one hand that's screaming "Freebird!" so make use of that freedom. Grab the loose yarn with your free hand. Take the loose yarn and pull it between the two needles in a diagonal motion away from your body. Loop the yarn around and behind the dominant-side needle. Now grasp that needle with your dominant hand while still holding the yarn.

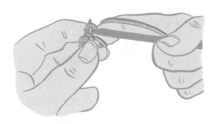

Step Four: *Pop it off!* Using the tip of the pointer finger on your submissive hand, push the tip of the dominant-hand needle toward your body. Then move that needle up and in front of the submissive-hand needle. There is now a single loop almost at the end of the submissive needle. Using the tip of the pointer finger on your submissive hand once again, push that loop off the tip of the needle and onto the tip of the dominant needle. Now you will have a loop on the once-bare dominant-hand needle. Tighten the loop with the loose yarn. Ta-da! You've knit your very first stitch! Continue repeating those steps until you've moved every stitch from one needle to the next. (And I mean move them by *knitting* them. It doesn't count if you just push them from one needle to the next with your hands.)

PURL!
(a.k.a. Knit in Reverse)

Purling is the yin to the yang of the knit stitch—it's the cream cheese to its bagel, it's the Sonny to its Cher (if Sonny and Cher had stayed together . . . man, if only they had stayed together). But when you come right down to it, purling is just a different way of making the stitch.

To purl, you enter the stitch from the front of the needle (instead of the back), and you pull the yarn from the front, not the back.

Step One: *Assume the position.* As always, start with your stitchy needle in your submissive hand and the bare needle in the dominant one.

Step Two: *Enter the purly gates.* Enter the loop from below the needle with the tip pointing away from your dominant hand.

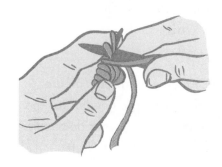

Step Three: *Grasp it!* Now grasp both needles in the vice grip of your submissive hand once again. Using your Freebird hand, pull the yarn up, around, and over the bare needle, easing in between the two needles and forming an upside-down U.

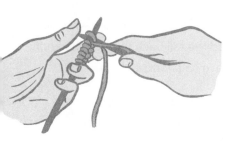

Step Four: *Pop it off.* Using your stitchy/submissive thumb, push with your thumb pad on the tip of the dominant-side needle, sliding the needle back toward your body so that the first part of the stitch slips off. Then push the dominant needle up and back behind the submissive one. Finally, pop the last part of the stitch off of your submissive needle with your pointer finger and onto the dominant needle. Wham, bam, thank you, hands! You've completed your very first purled stitch!

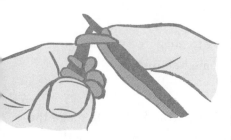

Repeat this series of steps until you've purled all of your stitches from one needle to the other.

CASTING OFF
(a.k.a. Sealing the Deal)

Step One: *Knit it.* Knit the first two stitches on your last row. The stitches will now be on your dominant-side needle.

Step Two: *Grasp it.* Grasping the top of the first stitch in your dominant hand, pull it up and over the second stitch and under the tip of the dominant-side needle. Where there were two stitches, there is now one.

Step Three: *Go back, Jack, do it again.* Knit the third stitch off the submissive-side needle and on to the dominant-side needle. Pull the older stitch up and over the new stitch on the dominant-side needle. Keep repeating these steps until you only have one stitch left.

Step Four: *Put a knot in it.* Cut the remaining yarn loose from the ball of yarn. Give yourself a few inches of yarn tail to work with. Slide the needle out of the stitch, and feed the tail back through the knot, tying up the loose end. Voilà—you have knit yourself to success!

Then do a little dance. Why? Because you're victorious, that's why! Victory dances can be inserted into your knitting as often as you desire. If you ever feel that you have triumphed over crafting adversities, do a little dance. Hey, even if you don't feel triumphant, do a little dance. You deserve to shake it.

Before we go any further, I am going to enlighten you about some common kitting errors and share some helpful tips:

- **"Ply" refers to the number of twisted strands used to make the yarn.** A two-ply yarn has only two strands, making it very thin. Three-ply has three strands and, yeah, you guessed it, four-ply yarn has four strands. The more delicate the project, the fewer plies you'll want to work with. A big, thick sweater, on the other hand, could stand to have some extra plies.

- **Try not to split plies while knitting.** When your needle accidentally separates one of your strands from the others, you've split your plies. If you do split them, your knitting will appear to have a small defect where the ply splits.

- **While it is difficult to get around certain craft needs (purchasing the right type of canvas, having enough clay, buying needles of the right size), there are places where one has the ability to be inventive and be frugal.** If you need three-ply yarn but have skein upon skein of four-ply, fear not. There's no need to put your four-ply darlings out to pasture. Instead, schedule a prep session during which you can wrest the fourth ply from its friends, giving you the three-ply yarn that you desire. Now, I don't recommend doing this for an entire sweater or other similarly grand project, but for, say, belt making, you'll be able to save a little cash and not waste much time.

  Any prep task that requires little concentration can be done just about anywhere, from in front of the TV to sitting on the train. Of course, you can make it more fun by taking it to a bar or coffee shop and deplying your skein amongst friends and jukeboxes. Your companions won't mind if you're silently splitting threads—in fact, they may want to get in on the action. Just rock the "painting this fence is soooo fun" routine and you'll have your three-ply in no time.

- **Don't start your yarn from the outside end of the skein.** Pull the yarn from the inside end. If you pull it from the outside, it will get tangled up beyond recognition at some point in your knitting process.

- **When you cast on your very first stitch, leave yourself a tail of yarn to work with.** You will need it to weave into your knitting when you are done to give your project a neat and finished look. You can always cut the tail down if it is too long, but a tail that's too short will be difficult to work with.

- **When casting on as a beginner, go easy on yourself**. Don't tighten your knots so vigorously that you can't knit into them. Allowing yourself a little give will make your first few rows much easier to get into. Once you know what you're doing, you can cast on as tight as you like. But as a beginner, cut yourself a little yarn slack.

- **When you begin knitting a new row, the needle in your dominant hand should always be empty.**

- **Never forget your roots.** If you were purling on row 5, and then you had to go answer the doorbell and sign for a package containing the Creedence Clearwater Revival four-disc collection of their greatest hits, it goes without saying that you may have forgotten what you were doing by the time you return to your needles. (Creedence must be played upon receipt and must be valiantly rocked-out to.) So when you return to your needles, you may not know where to begin. Pick up your needles, look at them, and remember this: Whether knitting or purling, if you are stopped mid-row, the long arm of the yarn will always be dangling on the side of your dominant hand. And if you are knitting, it will be hanging toward the back of your piece, but if you are purling, it will dangle down in the front. If you are doing the stockinet stitch, a.k.a "knit one row, purl the next," the smooth side is the knit side and the ridgey, bumpy side is the purl. So based on those clues, figure out where your hands are supposed to go and pick yourself up, dust yourself off, and pick up knitting or purling all over again.

CRAFTY INTERLUDE:
Field Trips! Air, Inspirado, and a Good Pair of Needles

When I was planning for my knitting-themed Crafternoon, I started getting a lot of emails from knitting virgins. They were shy, they were naive, and they wanted guidance. What type of needles should they buy? What is the best yarn to learn on? How much should they spend? Where should they shop? When should they have the big talk with their boyfriend? I started out responding to each person individually, answering each question to the best of my ability, forwarding them along to my mom if I knew I couldn't tackle them, and finally, referring them to my favorite little knitting store in Brooklyn. But the questions kept coming. I felt like the Oracle at Delphi, if Delphi was the ancient center of knitting. Sadly, the working girl that I am simply lacked the time to answer all the questions. Then, I suddenly had a brainwave—why not just invite people to kick off our next Crafternoon at my favorite knitting store? This would give the crafters the opportunity to ask tons of questions, get a tactile tour of all sorts of wool, and buy the supplies they need. Plus, my mom and I could be there to lend a helping hand. So I sent out my Crafternoon email as noted earlier, and I told my crafters where to meet if they wanted to shop before the crafting began.

And shop they did.

Almost all of the folks who were knitting naïfs met us at the store. My mom and I showed them around, pointing out the wide variety of wool and needles. They found inspiration in the knit projects on the walls and the knowledge and enthusiasm of the employees. All of the Crafternooners were able to choose exactly what type of yarn and needles they wanted for their first projects—the right price, the right color, the right weight, and the right-sized needles to match. And not only did they end up with the perfect supplies, but they now also had the address of a great place to buy yarn.

Knowing a local place where you can buy great supplies makes the crafting experience just that much more exciting. As I mentioned before, I am a huge fan of old materials, but I love knowing that there are stores out there that can supply me with cool new materials. Plus, craft stores are excellent sources of inspiration and expertise. But some Crafternooners would prefer to reduce, reuse, and recycle their craft materials instead of buying anew. So, for Crafternoon inspiration without consumer participation, there are plenty of other options. Start your day with a field trip to a museum or gallery or another place of crafty interest. As a New Yorker, finding this sort of thing is just as easy as pie. But for the crafters who do not live in New York, fear not! There is certainly a local gallery or museum that might be of interest to your Crafternoon crew. Historical societies often act as caretakers for local landmarks, and those landmarks often display local crafts. Even small community colleges often have regular art shows. Or drive to a bigger city nearby and see what you can find. And what if you don't have any of that? What if you live on the tundra with nothing but love of the craft? Well, don't despair. Maybe one of your Crafternooners has a collection of something handcrafted, be it quilts or dolls or pottery. And lest we forget, nature is always a great muse. Nature is the mother of everything, including craft.

GREAT MOMENTS IN CRAFT HISTORY:
The Introduction of the Circular Needle

While those who knit at home may not fully grasp the importance of the circular needle (my mom is one of those people), the urban knitter who braves public transit certainly does. When working with traditional needles on a crowded subway, you pose a threat to yourself and your fellow commuters. And that is not okay. So rather than fearfully wrangling your pointy needles, praying the train doesn't stop short and send them into a fellow passenger's eyes, go circular. This tool is actually a semicircle, not a true circle, with needle points on either end. With the pointy tips in the firm grasp of your hands and nothing but a soft circle of yarn in your center, you'll find your fellow travelers offering you compliments on your craft instead of shooting you dirty looks. And doesn't that make you feel all warm inside when that happens? Yeah, the warmth of pride sure does beat the chill of fear.

KNITTING PROJECT NUMBER ONE:
ARM WARMERS

As I mentioned before, when I moved
back to NYC in 2002, I was broke as
a joke. I had moved to the city with an
apartment but no job. Note to the public:
When moving to the most expensive city
in the country, it is better to have a job
and no apartment than it is to have an
apartment and no job. But I had the opportunity to move in with my best friend
in the universe, Christine, so I had to
say yes. Anyway, having taken the cart-
before-the-horse approach to moving, I
was strapped for cash at all times.

When winter came around, I didn't have the spare cash-ola to
purchase a brand-new, warm-and-toasty winter coat, so I took
to wearing my mother's old leopard-print coat. This worked well
until mid-December, when the weather turned insanely, uncom-
fortably, unrelentingly freezing all the time. See, although the
coat was fashionable, it lacked the down component that takes
warmth to the next level. In addition to its severe lack of down, it
also featured the heat saboteur that is the three-quarter-length
sleeve. Even when I wore the coat with gloves, there was a sweet
spot where my skin and the freezing-cold air could rendezvous
and do bad things. No amount of long-sleeved layering had an im-
pact on this problem because the shirt or sweater sleeves would
ride up my arm with the power of friction. I had to do something
to address the problem. And the answer came to me in a crafty
dream: I could knit myself some wrist cuffs to extend the warmth
layer from the end of my coat sleeves down the length of my arm.

The minute I thought of it, I took to knitting myself a pair of warming cuffs. And they worked like a charm. So in homage to Necessity, the mother of Invention, I give you the Arm Warmer, a.k.a. the Arm Savior for the Long-Armed Wearer of Short-Armed Vintage Coats.

Supplies
One skein of three-ply yarn (washable wool for warmth and comfort), size 8 needles, yarn needle, scissors

Step One: Cast on. Cast on 30–40 stitches, leaving a long tail. Knit three rows and hold them against your wrist to see if your wrist will be covered. Pull out the stitches and start all over if you need more or less room.

Step Two: *Get knitty and not gritty.* Knit nine or more rows, depending on how big you want the cuff to be. I know, there's some room for variance in these instructions, but that's because you're creating a custom product. Enjoy the variance.

Step Three: *Cast off.* Seal the deal by casting off. When you cut the yarn loose, leave a long tail. Using a yarn needle (which is not a knitting needle but a large needle that resembles a sewing needle), stitch the two sides of your bracelet together and make a knot at the end. I recommend using loose, circular stitches so it's easy to pull the bracelet on and off. Start by stitching up into the opposite edge of the bracelet and then loop back down into the first edge, creating loose loops. Repeat until you've seamed your bracelet closed. I like to leave the tail hanging, but if you're not a fan of that look, you can weave the tails into the bracelet along the seam and then cut the yarn. Give yourself enough weaving room so the weaving won't pull out.

Step Four: *Decorate.* To make your cuffs maximally awesome, you might want to adorn them with baubles, bows, or beads. Or maybe you just want to use buttons. For the brown cuffers that I custom made, I added a slew of brown buttons in different shades and sizes. You could button up one side and bead another, or leave one side plain and make the other pretty as a pony with sequins and ribbons. Even appliqué on knit looks pretty cool—you could appliqué LOVE on one cuff and HATE on the other, as a shout-out to *Night of the Hunter* and *Do the Right Thing* in two cinematic arm warmers. Or you could turn the Love/Hate thing on its head and just appliqué Craft/Love. Yeah, you know what? That reflects the spirit of Crafternoon more accurately. But however you make these cuffs your own, your arms will be glad they have them. A crafty arm is a healthy arm.

KNITTING PROJECT NUMBER TWO:
SKINNY MINI KNIT NECKLACE

Sometimes projects are born of necessity, while other times they are born of available materials and a desire to craft. Before my father retired, he worked in New York City's garment district as a yarn salesman, selling yarn from the manufacturers to the sweater makers. In the 1980s, my dad focused on the sale of metallic novelty yarn. When I was a kid, I remember going to his office and seeing piles and piles of yarn spools, the shiny yarn bright and ready to be shown to his best customers. This yarn was used in sweaters with big shoulder pads and big designs, worn by ladies with big hair. Most of the business went away in the 1990s, when it was no longer financially viable to make yarn in South Carolina and manufacture your garments in Brooklyn. So the yarn business slowly died out, but my dad kept a few spools of yarn lying around the house as souvenirs.

My mom stumbled across a few skeins of this yarn recently and passed them along to me. I was beyond excited. I had black and gold yarn and gold and white yarn, and I was free to do whatever I pleased with them. I knew I wanted to make something that played up the night-time disco appeal, so I settled on a simple design: a skinny scarf knit with big needles, which create plenty of air and space, just like an astronaut museum. This scarf can also be finished to create the skinny scarf's überhip cousin, the knit necklace.

Supplies
One skein of two- or three-ply yarn (metallic, if available), size 15 (circular: optional) needles, yarn needle, scissors

Find a cool, lightweight yarn. Ideally, something in a two or three ply will work best, and something shiny will make it more fun. You'll be casting on five stitches using a size 15 or larger circular needle. Yup, just five stitches—remember, this is going to be skinny mini!

Step One: Cast on five little stitches.

Step Two: Knit 80–90 rows.

Step Three: Cast off.

Step Four: To finish the scarf, tie off your final stitch, then weave the ends of your yarn into the ends of the scarf. Voilà, you are all set to rock out skinny style!

To finish the textile necklace, tie off your final stitch. When you cut the yarn, give yourself a nice, long tail to work with. Flatten the scarf completely on a bed or another large surface, making sure there are no twists or knots in the piece. Then take the ends of the piece and bring them together, forming a complete circle. Knot each tail to the opposite end of the knitting. Using a yarn needle, seam the ends together using one of the tails. Tie off each tail after seaming, then weave the rest of the tails through the end of the piece. You have your necklace! You can wear it as is or double it over for a different look. It'll be the crown of your jewels!

KNITTING PROJECT NUMBER THREE: KNIT COASTERS

Supplies
One skein of three-ply washable yarn, size 8 needles, yarn needle, scissors

It's fun to make wearable knit gifts for your friends, but what do you do when you've made more skinny mini knit necklaces and arm extenders than you can count? You need to switch it up and make something for the home instead. After all, variety is the spice of life, and you are one spicy meatball. So I say, kick your knitting into furniture protection mode and knit your friends some hip coasters!

Even though I love old, worn-in furniture, I'm not a big fan of water stains. Now, I'm sure there are some folks out there who really love a solid water stain on a piece of furniture. In this crazy, mixed-up world we live in, people pay a premium for jeans that are expertly "distressed" in factories: brand-new jeans that get pounded with rocks and rubbed with heavy-duty nail files to look like they are worn in and have character, giving the garment a false appearance of aging. Man, I can't wait until the rest of our culture is really into aging! Do you think people will start injecting their faces with things to give themselves *more* wrinkles? And cosmetically adding sunspots? I wouldn't put it past us.

So, if you've got friends who love the character a water stain provides, don't bother knitting them some cute coasters. They'll just hide them away in a drawer somewhere. But most anyone else would be happy to get a cute, cozy knit coaster. Knit your coaster tightly, and it will keep the water off of any table.

Step One: Using size 8 needles and three-ply yarn, cast on 16 stitches.

Step Two: Knit one row.

Step Three: Purl the next row.

Step Four: Continue switching between knitting rows and purling rows until you have completed 12 rows.

Step Five: Cast off row 12 and knot the final stitch. Cut a tail and weave it into the knit piece. Now you're coasting!

Knit yourself silly, dear crafters! And while I should warn you that this craft can be addictive, I think you'll forgive me. A habit that's addictive and relaxing is hard to come by these days, so grab your knitting needles and get your crafty fix.

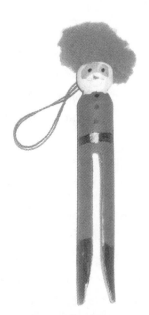

CHAPTER TWELVE

DECEMBER

HARBINGERS OF THE HOLIDAYS

When Madonna sang, "Holiday! Celebrate!" she really knew what she was talking about. The season to be jolly, to deck the halls, to ding-dong merrily on high, to make things out of clay, and to give partridges in pear trees is definitely worthy of celebrating. And for those of us who dwell in climates with four distinct seasons, the weather outside *is* frightful. But the crafting is so delightful! And it's no coincidence that the most wonderful time of the year is also the craftiest. If you're a fan of gift giving and a fan of craft, you make a list and check it twice, and then decide who gets what handmade treasure.

But the craftiest time of the year is also the busiest. The holiday nights fill up with parties and recitals, and the days are spent prepping and decorating and shop-'til-you-drop-ing. Suddenly that list of gifts to make can seem less fun and more overwhelming. How can you fit all the crafting you need to do into your busy social calendar? You can throw a Holiday Crafternoon, that's how! Gee, you should have seen that coming from a mile away.

Your Holiday Crafternoon will be the hit of the social calendar. I guarantee that most of your crafty friends will also have bitten off more than they can craft, and a social event with a crafting element will be a total godsend. Nothing like killing two birds with one stone during the holiday season. And a daytime event that focuses more on handiwork and less on drink specials will be a welcome change of pace. Yes, Crafternoon has been known to cure hangovers. No, I haven't figured out how to bottle it—just how to commit it to paper.

"Sounds great," you say with a smile. But your brow furrows once again in seconds flat. "Wait a minute! Throwing a party is a lot of work! I've already got too much work to do! If I spend my time prepping for this Crafternoon, when will I knit those socks for Bobby and pickle those beets for Aunt Carol and get myself a new shirt for the company party? I can't do any of that if I'm tied to the kitchen, wrapping little pigs into their cozy blankets of deliciousness and hand rolling the dough for a hundred mini pizzas. . . ."

Whoa, there, Captain Overwhelm. Who said anything about pigs in blankets and hand-rolled mini pizzas? You're forgetting that Crafternoon is the most low-key party you can throw, no matter what time of year it is. So while other holiday gatherings would have the host whipping up platter upon platter of delicate hors d'oeuvres, Crafternoon is always a potluck of good times. And to put a new twist on an old potluck tradition, encourage your crafters to bring a holiday treat that's a family tradition. Your crafters will happily oblige, and I'm betting you'll wind up with a deliciously eclectic menu.

GET THE WORD OUT AND SET UP YOUR SPACE

Here's the note I sent through the Web to get my crafters going. I hope it sparks a warm holiday feeling inside your crafty heart:

> *Sleigh bells ring and the weather outside is frightful, so deck the halls with crafty goodies for the holidays! This Sunday at 1 p.m., please join me for a Crafternoon of holiday goodness. We'll be making holiday cards using a variety of techniques, making clothespin ornaments to trim your tree or decorate your menorah, and generally making merry while crafting the afternoon away.*
>
> *This is our very first Manhattan Crafternoon, and the hostess is my wonderful friend Emilie. We will welcome any materials that folks want to bring along for the crafting of holiday cards or ornaments. And remember, the holidays are a time for chowing down, so please bring a treat to contribute to the Crafternoon cornucopia. Cookies, cakes, fruits, chips, dips, cheeses, beverages, crudités—you name it, we'll eat it!*
>
> *And, as always, you are welcome to BYOP—Bring Your Own Project! I know that many of us have special things we are working on for the holidays. Feel free to bring that half-knit scarf along for the ride.*
>
> *Yours in Crafternoon camaraderie,*
>
> *Maura*

For sustenance during my Holiday Crafternoon, I broke out my mom's spiced pecans. They used to be a holiday-only extravagance, but they are so irresistible that she started making them the whole year through. Here's the recipe, but I warn you: Once you pop, you can't stop.

TREAT OF THE 'NOON:
Pam Madden's Spiced Pecans

2 egg whites, room temperature
½ teaspoon cinnamon
½ teaspoon cocoa
1 teaspoon salt
1 cup sugar
4 cups pecans

Preheat the oven to 250°F, and spray a cookie sheet with a non-stick coating. In a large bowl, beat the egg whites lightly. Then add the cinnamon, cocoa, salt, and sugar, stirring until blended. Add the pecans to the mix, stirring to coat the pecans evenly. Place the pecans on the baking sheet, distributing them evenly. Bake for approximately 1 hour, turning the pecans every 20 minutes until the liquid is absorbed. Remove from the oven and cool. Store the pecans in a tin.

And here's a bonus recipe, just for the heck of it. This is something my mom still reserves for the holidays only. Her quintessential holiday treat is dates filled with peanut butter and sprinkled with coconut. This was her father's favorite Christmas goodie, and it's a tasty one. Just pit the dates, stuff them with a dab of peanut butter, and sprinkle them with dried coconut. My mouth is watering just thinking about them.

RECIPE PARTY: A BINDER OF HOLIDAY TREATS

Presents are the focus of so many holiday gatherings, but sharing will be the focus of your Crafternoon. Why not take the potluck concept to the next level of sharing and create a memento of your first year of Crafternoon? Ask everyone to bring enough copies of their holiday recipe to share with other crafters. And ask them all to bring them in a binder, a folder, or a notebook. Crafters can put their recipes on a central table, and all of the attendees can grab a copy of each recipe to add to their Holiday Crafternoon cookbook. My mom has been doing this sort of recipe-sharing thing at work functions for a while, and people always seem to get really excited about it. (Although famous chefs may not be willing to share their best recipes, most folks are flattered to have someone ask for their secret ingredient. And why be greedy with a great treat? If you're going to become the next Colonel at Kentucky Fried Chicken, then by all means keep your recipes close to your heart. But if you've got no intention to go into the restaurant business, then why keep a good formula all to yourself? Huh?) Start that New Year's resolution to share more by doing this. You'll get a head start and a gold star.

Holiday Crafternoon will be a lot of things for a lot of people. The crafty go-getters you know will bring along their holiday gift projects and get down to work. The crafty folks with less of a plan will appreciate the opportunity to bang out a few gifts in a few hours. To that end, your Holiday Crafternoon projects should be easy to complete in one afternoon. Holiday time is not the time to start a long, complicated project, and having some handmade items to bring home will give your crafters a satisfying sense of completion. And completion is a rare feeling during the holiday season but a good one nonetheless.

HOLIDAY PROJECT NUMBER ONE:
HAND-STAMPED WRAPPING PAPER

One project that is sure to please is the hand-stamped wrapping paper project. Try saying that three times fast. When I was a kid, my mom stumbled across this project, and we enjoyed it so thoroughly that we stamped our way to unique holiday wrapping a few years in a row.

Supplies
Kraft paper (a.k.a. butcher paper), Stryofoam trays, chopstick or pencil, scissors, sponges, water-based acrylic paints

Step One: *Prepare the trays.* Cut the curved edges off the Styrofoam trays so that the flat surface can be pressed directly on the paper. I'm sure you would have figured out this step, but I don't want to leave out any key details.

Step Two: *Create the stamps.* Styrofoam trays can be treated like linocut surfaces if you use a chopstick or a pencil with a dull point to carve the design onto the surface. Because these lines won't receive the ink when it comes time to press, they will create negative space, or the appearance of lines. It's a nice little effect, and it manages to make an ornament look more like an ornament and less like an unidentified blob. (I mean, it's not that I don't like a good Christmas blob, but there are some folks out there who are picky.) Using a chopstick or dull pencil, draw shapes on some of the trays, such as trees, ornaments, angels, wreaths, stockings, candy canes, and Santa Clauses. Then cut along the edges of the designs with heavy-duty scissors to create your stamps. You can also use this carving technique to draw a complete scene to stamp on paper or a card. Try tracing a simple image from a book or magazine and then taping the image to your tray and carving it in.

For a stamp with a different look, my mom brought along some sponges that we cut into the shapes of stars and Christmas stockings. There's something nice about the squishiness of a sponge. The downside to sponge stamps is their lack of subtlety—it's hard to generate sweet details in a sponge format, and the image really looks like it was made by a sponge (which makes sense because it *was* made by a sponge).

Step Three: *Dip it!* Fill the extra Styrofoam trays with paint, and dip the stamps into the trays to ink them.

Step Four: *Stamp it!* With your paint-dipped stamps, start marking up your kraft paper. Once you've stamped to your heart's content, set the paper out to dry. Voilà—instantly awesome wrapping paper!

HOLIDAY PROJECT NUMBER TWO: CHRISTMAS BAGEL ORNAMENTS

No holiday craft party would be complete without an ornament-making extravaganza. When I was a kid, my mom experimented with a few different ornament-making styles and techniques, but these are the two that she still uses to this day: the Christmas Bagel and the Clothespin Doll. The Christmas Bagel is easy to make and always good for a smile. The Clothespin Doll is more time-consuming and labor intensive but offers the opportunity for endless variations. Here are instructions on how to make both of them.

Supplies
Mini bagels (See if your local bagel shop has them; if not, most grocery stores have them in their freezer section), scrap paper, red and green felt-tip pens, clear nail polish (easier to find than shellac and does the same job), red or green ribbon, glue, scissors

Note to crafters! If you decide to make Christmas Bagels, plan ahead! The mini bagels are much easier to work on when they are stale since they achieve a rock-solid consistency that makes them easier to draw on. Give them a day or two in a paper bag to get nice and firm and then do your decorating. If you're using frozen bagels, let them thaw and then harden. The effect will be the same.

Step One: *Practice drawing ivy leaves.* On a piece of scrap paper, practice your ivy artistry. It's really simple, but you might as well try it out a few times before you put pen to bagel.

Step Two: *Get the ivy on the bagel!* Put your bagel down on a surface where it will not slip. I recommend a little piece of felt. Draw ivy leaves around the bagel with the green pen. Then go back and add little red holly berries here and there. Let the ink dry for a minute or two.

Step Three: *Seal it with a kiss (of nail polish).* You've decked the bagel with boughs of holly and ivy—but you don't want your handiwork to rub off on anyone. Paint one side of your bagel with a clear coat of nail polish. Let it dry, then paint the other.

Step Four: *Hang it up.* Cut a piece of ribbon 4–5 inches long. Tie it around the top of the bagel, then make a loop to hang it from, and voilà! You've got your Christmas bagel.

HOLIDAY PROJECT NUMBER THREE:
CLOTHESPIN DOLLS!

Clothespin dolls have existed in the United States since colonial times, when kids would steal clothespins to make little wooden dolls with no arms. That's right, armless dolls were a hot commodity back then. Man, colonial times were hard. Anyway, my mom went to a Christmas craft fair way back in the 1970s, and she saw someone selling soldier ornaments made out of clothespins. She then started making her own clothespin ornaments as Christmas gifts, creating two prototypes that were fun to make and always well received—the angel and the Santa Claus. She also created her own version of the soldier boy, a favorite with the young lads.

When my friend Emilie hosted a holiday Crafternoon at her house two years ago, my mom brought a bag of clothespins and some acrylic paints and everyone made their own clothespin dollies. Emilie was married in Coney Island on the day of the Mermaid Parade, so she decided to make herself a clothespin mermaid. My best friend, Christine, was getting married that February, so my mom was working on clothespin bride and groom dolls for the top of her wedding cake. Mom also whipped up a clothespin ballerina doll wearing a red leotard for my very own Christmas tree. My brother's girlfriend, Emmy, made a little angel with a tulle skirt and wings, as well as a Santa Claus with cotton for a beard and a little red fabric cone hat with a cotton tip. Also there were my friends Samara and Linda, who made cards, and my friend Trey who mainly kicked it. (If the above projects didn't inspire you, well, you could also make a punk rocker, an art star, a butcher, a baker, a candlestick maker, an IT dude, a policeman, a fireman, a movie star getting out of rehab—any character your little heart desires. All it takes is a little paint, a little fabric, and some imagination.)

Supplies
Wooden clothespins (without wire if available), acrylic paint (in several colors), embroidery floss (in several colors including black, yellow, brown, and red for hair color, as well as a neutral color to use to hang the ornaments), fabric scraps (including tulle if making angels, brides, ballerinas, or other fans of tulle), ribbon (can be used instead of or in addition to fabric scraps), glue, scissors, small paintbrushes

Step One: *Paint your wagon! Er, clothespin . . .* Yup, the clothespin's got the figure that you're looking for, but now you need a face. Paint it on! If you enjoy prep work, you can draw the face on with pencil and then paint over it. I am terrible at painting the face on because it requires a delicate touch, and I lack the delicacy gene. I usually commission my mother to paint the face, then I take it from there. I do hand the clothespin right back to my mom if I need more detailing, though. Man, you should see what she does on low riders! So, paint the face, the hair, and the clothes right on the clothespin. If you are going to add elements such as a mermaid tail cut from fabric, you can paint some underwear on the gal. Just because she lives under the sea doesn't mean she has to act like a rehab-ready celebrity and forget her undies. If you are painting layers of different colors, let the first color dry before you begin painting on the second. Am I overstating the obvious? Better to craft safe than craft sorry.

Step Two: _Add-ons._ One summer I worked at a large retail clothing chain. The managers explained that one important sales technique was the Add-On (their capitals, not mine). This is the part of the sale when you convince the customers that although they already have a ton of stuff, there are a few great deals that will make their shopping trip the best ever. This sales technique could also have been called, "Sell them socks," but I guess that didn't sound like corporate speech. Similarly, "add-ons" refers to the part of the clothespin doll-making process where you add on elements to make your doll complete. For instance:

Santa Claus: Glue a loop of red embroidery thread to the top of Santa's head and then top it with a red pom-pom.

Ballerina: Cut a circle out of tulle or the fabric of your choice. This will be your skirt. Then fold the circle in half and carefully cut another circle in the center of that circle. The clothespin will fit through this hole. It should be a tight fit so that the fabric will stay up on its own volition. You could use a ribbon instead, but you will need to gather the ribbon around your clothespin using a running stitch (with a needle and thread).

Step Three: *Leave it well hung.* Loop the thread of floss around the doll's neck or glue it to its back or head if you feel too weird about the neck loop. And bam—you are holiday-tastic!

These projects all make great gifts, but how about a little something for your very own abode? Maybe a gingerbread house. Who doesn't want one of those? My mom always made a gingerbread house when I was little. She would put together the base (walls, roof), and my brother and I would each invite a friend over to decorate it with icing and candy. (Decorating with candy is quite popular with kids.) But my mom wanted to send our friends home with sweet houses of their very own, so she came up with the idea for a faux-gingerbread house. I share the recipe with you now.

PAM MADDEN'S FAUX-GINGERBREAD (ACTUALLY GRAHAM CRACKER) HOUSE!

Icing
1 egg white, room temperature
1 ½ cups confectioners' sugar
½ teaspoon cream of tartar

House
Paper plates, small
One 14.4-ounce box of graham crackers
Brown construction paper
Scissors
Candy: red licorice, gumdrops, candy canes, chocolate Santas, nonpareils, hard candies (basically any candy that you want to see on and around your sweet house)

Making the snow (icing). In a bowl, beat the egg white for about 1 minute until it gets foamy. Gradually add the sugar and cream of tartar, and beat until the ingredients are completely mixed together and little peaks form. Cover immediately with plastic wrap or a dampened cloth. This icing begins to harden super-quickly, so you must work fast and always cover your bowl.

Building your candy dream house. Take a paper plate and cover it with icing. Break a graham cracker in half so you are left with two squares. Stick the squares into the icing so they form an L shape, then seal the corner with some more icing. Repeat that step to complete a square. Now place another graham-cracker square on top of the house, cementing it in place with icing.

Cut a rectangle out of a piece of brown construction paper, ⅛-inch longer and slightly skinnier than a whole graham cracker. Snap cracker in half. Coat the paper with icing, and attach the cracker squares, leaving a ⅛-inch gap between the two squares. Now add it to the house like the roof of a deck of cards, securing it with more icing. When dry, frost the roof completely and decorate it with candy while the icing is wet. And voilà—you've got your very own gingerbread home!

CRAFTERNOON

HOLIDAY PROJECT NUMBER FOUR:

DREIDEL, DREIDEL, DREIDEL!

As most of us know from the dreidel song, a standard dreidel is made out of clay. So what are you waiting for? Grab some of your leftover Fimo and get cracking!

Supplies
Fimo clay (one color or many), carving implement, oven

Step One: Get clayful. Mush and knead your clay until it's in molding condition. For a cool dreidel, smush multiple clay colors together for a swirled look. Form the clay into a squarish shape with a pointy bottom. Then flatten the square carefully on each side, and roll the pointy bottom around the tabletop until it is sharp enough to be spun upon.

Step Two: Lettering. On each side, carefully draw these four Hebrew letters with your carving tool in succession: nun, gimel, hey, and shin. When you are done, bake it, let it dry, and oh, dreidel, I shall play!

Whatever holiday you're celebrating, your Holiday Crafternoon will help you seal the deal on a crafty year of good times and great crafting.

the **CRAFTERNOON** catchall

COMPONENTS OF A SUCCESSFUL CRAFTERNOON

For starters, the main component of a great Crafternoon is the right mix of crafters. Just like a good party, a good Crafternoon relies on an enthusiastic and interactive group of friendlies. Invite loads of people because the more, the better, but if you're going to open your home to the masses, you've got to be ready when the masses arrive. So let's say a new friend happens to bring an old nemesis along for the fun. So what? Suck it up. If the nemesis is a craft enthusiast, chances are there's something wonderful about him or her. So give him or her the Crafternoon benefit of the doubt and he or she just might surprise you.

When I meet people for the first time and I like them, I tell them about Crafternoon. That's all there is to it. I don't grill them on their craft background, nor do I test their origami skills with the phone bill in my bag. I just tell them about it and see if they want to come. There are people whom I have had on my list for more than a year who have only come once, maybe eight months into receiving my invites. And did they have a good time when they came? Hell, yes! And was I happy to see them crafting? Of course! Even if they only craft it up once, I'm thrilled to have them.

FIVE WEIRDOS CRAFTING

At the moment, I am happy to have lots of friends on my Crafternoon list, and the Crafternoons are quite full of many friends. But there is no reason why your Crafternoon has to be a big gathering. Small Crafternoons can be just as beautiful.

Sometimes Crafternoon just ends up being small, even when you thought it was going to be big. This can be wonderful, but I'll admit that it can also be a bit awkward. These are the Crafternoons that I refer to as "Five Weirdos Crafting." I am, of course, including myself in the weirdo category. There have been times when the planets and the social calendars align in such a way that my mass Crafternoon email yields a turnout of my mom, my mom's friend, somebody's friend from work, and one good friend of mine. This can make for some odd crafting, but you gotta embrace the strange. As host/ess of Crafternoon, no one should ever leave your place feeling less than outrageously welcome.

GROUP CLEANUPS

For the first two years of Crafternoon, I took on the responsibility of cleaning up after my fellow crafters. Crafternoon is usually a casual thing, with the day often seeping into the night and late crafters often breathing new life into an otherwise winding down Crafternoon. I often had a hand or two to help the cleaning go more swiftly, but I usually took on the greater part of the responsibility, in my role as Crafternoon hostess/cleanup martyr. And then, one day in January, I had a Crafternoon conundrum.

I was hosting Crafternoon at a friend's house in Brooklyn in the afternoon (when else?). But as it turned out, I had to be in Manhattan in the early part of the evening. I thought that I had given myself plenty of time to craft and clean and then travel to my evening event, but as the Crafternoon continued, I could see that I was going to be cutting it close. And with the mess now made at the house of a friend, I couldn't just leave it and deal with it when I got home. And so, embarrassed as could be, I decided that I would have to make an announcement that Crafternoon was coming to a close. I begged everyone's forgiveness for my hostessing faux pas and explained that I simply needed a chance to clean before leaving for my second event.

But something kickass happened next. See, when I told my friends that I needed to clean, they all decided to help clean with me. And just as everyone had been pitching in with suggestions and materials and craft genius for hours before, they now sprang into action, cleaning my friend's apartment shoulder to shoulder with me. And with 15 people pitching in to clean, we left his house cleaner than it had been when we got there. From that point on, I realized that the group cleanup is key to Crafternoon. Because cleaning up is part of the process. Just like craft time in kindergarten always ended with a big group cleaning, Crafternoon ought to end with cooperative tidying up. The mess of craft is the responsibility of the whole Crafternoon community, not just little-old-me or little-old-you.

And group cleanups are fun! There is a satisfaction that comes from helping out, from taking the mess you made and helping to put everything back in its place. Crafternoon is about creation, but it's also about caring for your crafty space. So like they say, campers, you want to leave it as you found it. And that is everyone's responsibility.

TURNING A PLAIN OLD CRAFTERNOON INTO "CRAFTERNOON: THE BIRTHDAY PARTY!"

Crafternoon is really the perfect kids' party idea. I'm not trying to sound arrogant, but it's flawless. When children gather in a group to celebrate one another's birthdays, madness is usually on the menu. Children in a group + cake + presents = virtual insanity. No, wait, it = literal insanity. Nothing virtual about a children's birthday party—they are full-on, in-your-face occasions filled with wild behavior. Because of this tendency toward craziness, children's birthday parties often become the dreaded appointment on the parental social calendar. But it need not be so, mothers and fathers of the world! Make your kid's next birthday party a Crafternoon, and you will find yourself hosting a festive occasion marked by creativity, civility, and calm. Kids and parents alike enjoy settling down for a few hours of creating and cake eating.

Don't believe me? I have proof (and witnesses). A few years back, my friend Marie hosted a Crafternoon birthday party for her daughter Madeline, and it was a smashing success. Madeline was turning seven at the time, and I've never seen such a stress-free children's birthday party. All the kids were on the floor painting and gluing and sharing supplies and concentrating, and there were no hissy fits or spontaneous relay races in Marie's New York apartment. It was all concentration and collaboration. Who could ask for anything more? To transform your Crafternoon into a Crafternoon: The Birthday Party!, follow a few simple steps:

Send out paper invitations instead of emails. I recommend getting a little crafty with your invites—even if you just make some simple potato stamps of balloons and birthday cakes and stamp the heck out of some card stock, making a card will set the tone for the party. And the party is all about making stuff, so make something, why don't ya?

Purchase all the supplies yourself. Since it's a party, you should provide the food, drink, and supplies on your own. If you disagree, feel free to potluck it up. I'm not going to stop you, though I will say that you've been warned.

Bake a crafty cake. Make it from scratch, and decorate it, too! Use cookies to doll it up with crafty shapes, or if you're a whiz with an icing pen, draw yourself a crafty little scene.

Pummel a piñata! It's true that piñatas really rile kids (and adults) up, but after crafting quietly and eating cake, they're going to want to expend some energy. In fact, if you don't give them a papier-mâché target, they may find a target of their own that you'd be less happy with. Yes, that Precious Moments collection you received from your mother-in-law may take a bit of a beating at the hands of some cake-filled children. For some people, that might be fine, but for others, that would spell disaster. Might just be better to have a piñata on hand and call it a day. You can buy a piñata, but in the spirit of craftiness, it might be more fun to make your own. Follow the papier-mâché instructions in the Halloween chapter on page 162. Instead of just covering the front of the balloon, cover the entire balloon in gooey strips. Let it dry 24 hours, then cut a trapdoor at the bottom of the balloon using an X-Acto blade. Pop the balloon and pull it out. Turn the orb upside down so that the trapdoor will be at the top. Then paint the piñata or decorate it with tissue paper to make it look fun. Fill it with party favors, turn it upside down, seal the trapdoor with glue, and hang it from the ceiling. And when the time comes, smash it.

Do me a party favor. If you want to take your Crafternoon: The Birthday Party! to the next level, you can send your guests home with a sweet party favor. Here are some suggestions:

• **A to-go kit** with all the supplies needed to tackle the craft of the afternoon at your guest's very own home. For example, if you were hosting the knitting Crafternoon, you could give your guests a skein of yarn and a pair of needles. Tie it with a ribbon, and if you are feeling generous, loop a yarn needle into your bow so they'll have all the necessary tools at the ready. Make the kit even more practical and unique by handwriting or typing up instructions for the craft and including them with each kit.

• **A reusable tote bag** is a great and cool way to show the planet you care. Tote bags can be purchased in bulk online and then decorated with a silkscreen of your own design, photos of friends and family, appliqués, sequins, or fabric details. The simplest customizations can turn a simple bag into a knock-out. Heck, you could even just stencil the word "Crafternoon" on the side of the bag and call it a day. You know, get the good word out there.

- **Gift cards to your local craft store.** Now, I'm not a huge fan of giving out items that obviously state their monetary value, but I understand that sometimes life gets in the way of the best-laid craft projects. Find out if your local craft store offers certificates, and figure out an amount you see fit to multiply by the number of party guests. Then buy those certificates. You'll be contributing to future craft projects.

THINK GLOBALLY, SHOP LOCALLY!

Many suburban areas have both little craft stores and large craft emporiums where there are knowledgeable staff people. Just go and ask the manager who the craftiest person on staff is. When you find that person, explain what you are attempting to undertake and the level of skill that you have in that area. Chances are good that he or she will be able to help you gauge if it is an appropriate project for you and your Crafternoon group.

In urban areas, there are fewer giant craft stores, but there is usually an abundance of specialty craft stores. Go to the store that supplies crafts most akin to the project you are embarking on. For example, for the bargello project, I'd hit my local needlepoint store or knitting zone. For people who like to work with yarn, the leap from knitting to needlepoint is not a large one, and the chances are good that you'll find some needlepoint enthusiasts at the store to give you pointers about bargello. And if they don't know how to rock the barge, they might know where to direct you.

. . . BACK TO YOUR REGULARLY SCHEDULED CRAFTERNOON: HOW TO CREATE THE CRAFTY MOOD

Single flowers in tall, slender vases work well when decorating for a Crafternoon. If you want to spice up a cylindrical vase with a little decoration, wrap it with a page from an old magazine. For a tight fit, wrap the empty vase with the paper and cut the paper to fit the vase. Then tape the underside of the overlapping paper so that it lies flat. If you want a cleaner look, you can buy a nice sheet of handmade paper to wrap the vase with. You could choose any color, really—whatever feels festive to you and works with your décor. Cut the paper, tape it to fit, then take a small piece of raffia and tie it around the outside of the vase. Carefully fill the vase with water and drop in your flowers. This will look very classy indeed. If you're looking to add some favors to your crafting party, make enough wrapped vases so that everyone can take one home. To be thrifty, try to make nice with your florist a few weeks in advance and see if they'll order a box of vases for you: They should be able to get a discount.

MAKE A MIX TAPE!

Now, I know some people like to sit and craft in silence, but not me. I like to get the music pumping and get my crafters going. After all, the whole idea behind Crafternoon is creating a crafting environment that's got a party feel. So put on some sweet tunes! Me, I like the jams that have the quick tempo and the awesome melodies. If you prefer the classical to the rock, then feel free to take your friends on a classical journey, or any musical journey that you think will appeal. I like to make a mix that will last for a few hours so I can put it on and not think about it. I also like to include a few songs that allude to the craft of the day. You can choose a musical theme, too: love songs for your valentine

Crafternoon, American rock anthems for Freedom Craft, country-western songs for your quilting Crafternoon. But if you're not into themes, just throw a bunch of your favorite tunes on a playlist and call it a day. Or get the Led out and let Jimmy Page and Robert Plant do all the work. Man, if I could have anyone in the world write a Crafternoon theme song, you can bet all of my love that it would be those two gentlemen of rock.

I don't blast my crafters out of their seats volume-wise, but I find that good tunes played at even a low level add some extra energy and excitement to any Crafternoon. And talk about icebreakers—mix tapes give people the perfect excuse to talk to each other. When folks love the same songs, they've got something to talk about. When folks hate the same song, they have something even better to talk about. Though please note that it is not polite to complain about the host's choice in music. You could gently remark upon the volume if you find that it is too loud, but dissing it altogether is not okay. Nor is it polite to commandeer the boom box and replace your host's mix tape with a selection of experimental jazz. If you want to contribute some tunes, get clearance from your host before you do so. It goes both ways, of course—as host, you should try to accommodate your guests' needs and respect their eardrums. So if you find that the bands you've chosen to play are making some of your guests craft their own earplugs, you might want to switch it up to something less aggressive. A good guest doesn't rock the boat, and a good host makes sure there is no reason for the boat to be rocking.

SPACECRAFT! CREATING A CRAFTING SPACE IN YOUR VERY OWN PLACE

Sometimes it's fun to have your own one-person Crafternoon at the drop of a hat. And even the busiest among us can make time for a little crafting. Just like the cardio you're supposed to fit in three times a week, a few minutes of crafting a few times a week can turn a normal week into a craftastic one. But being able to craft at a moment's notice requires a certain number of supplies and tools on hand. Whether you're a knitter or a collage artist or a metalworker, if you can set aside a little permanent space for crafting, you'll be more likely to craft whenever you're feeling the fever.

My friend Lori, for example, has got the ideal SpaceCraft, and she's always whipping up the coolest handmade creations. Lori has a whole section of her apartment dedicated to crafting. Like so many New Yorkers (myself included), she lives in a railroad-style apartment. Each room goes directly into the next, following a straight path just like cars on a train. Her front room is her bedroom, which also has a living room space. Her back room is her kitchen. And in the middle, there's a space that serves as her craft haven. She has drawers and drawers of craft supplies, all perfectly organized, a space for her sewing machine, and a table just for crafting. She even has bookshelves in there to display her creations and hold even more craft supplies. Everything has its place in Lori's craft room. She's living the crafty dream.

In my own house, disorganization used to reign supreme in the craft realm. Craft supplies were spread out all over the place, tucked into any available nook or cranny, like jam on so many crafty English muffins. When I wanted to make a last-minute collage card for someone's birthday or embroider a little something on a shirt, I had to dig through piles of things to get to the raw materials. And when piles are disturbed, they often fall apart and create new piles. That's how piles reproduce! So the piles would spill out into little piles all over the place, and before I could get down to my crafting, I had to spend time cleaning up the mess. After spending those minutes or (sometimes) hours playing pile-wrangler, one of two things would happen: Either I would no longer have time in my busy day to fit in my moment of crafting, or I would start crafting in something of a foul mood. Crafting in a foul mood is just silly. It really goes against the whole purpose of crafting if you're sitting in your house, muttering bitterly to yourself while applying glitter to something. Whenever I had my pile fights, I would start my crafting like an angry lion. It's much better to craft when you're feeling like a happy little lamb.

Inspired by Lori and the desire to craft happy, Rufus and I recently decided to attack Pile City. We rented a car and took a trip outside of the city limits to one of those colossal Scandinavian furniture stores (these stores are the stuff of legend, and with good reason), and we invested in some tools to organize our life. We got all sorts of things, like coat hooks and cupboard dividers and pot holders and napkins. It's hard not to get sucked in by the low, low prices. But the pièce de résistance was the small, assembly required dresser that seems custom made for holding art supplies. There's a drawer for almost everything—one for Rufus's paints, one for paper products, one for pens and markers, one for scissors and other craft tools, one for the supplies for the silk-screened posters and flyers that we make for our variety show, and one that's a crafting catchall.

Our dining room is now a craft center that can be converted back to a dining room on a moment's notice. Rufus has hung bulletin boards up on the wall above it, which has proven to be a great place to display works in progress and postcards and old family photos. This little craft zone has made our apartment a kinder, craftier place to live in and to visit.

SUPPLIES FOOTNOTE:
EVERYTHING IN ITS RIGHT PLACE

This year I put all the valentine-making materials in a big pile on the table in my dining room/craft room. This seemed like the right idea at the time, since I figured most folks would end up sitting around the table, and they could just grab at stuff in the center. That's how I've set the place up in the past, and it had always created a workspace of maximum convenience. But when the Valentine Crafternoon turnout was much larger than I had expected, getting to the pile in the center of the table became a somewhat awkward affair, since those who didn't come early enough to score VIP seating had restricted access to the materials. My friend Samara suggested that next time we set up a materials table in the corner of that room. That way, people could pick up materials and bring them back to their own workspace, without having to reach over people who were actively crafting.

The lesson? Don't let a materials bottleneck happen at your Crafternoon by putting your materials in a space with restricted access. Find a neutral, seat-free location and set your materials there. You can still have a small selection of materials and tools on the main table, but keep the bulk of the materials in an unoccupied space. Thinking about where to place your materials in advance will create flow and ensure that none of your Crafters feel velvet-roped off from the good stuff.

When it comes to the donations of sustenance, you still have to stay strategic. Distribute the food donations throughout the space so your crafters don't end up with tons of used plates and napkins cluttering up their workspace. Remember that part of your job as the host is making sure that everyone is fed and supplied and happy in your home. It drives me crazy when I go to someone's home and they don't offer me a beverage. I don't want to have to ask for one—that feels rude. But not offering one to your guests is rude, too. I try to make sure that crafters get their first beverage from me, and then I tell them to help themselves. This gives me a chance to connect with them as I pour them a glass, and I hope it makes them feel excited and ready for the rest of the 'noon. Have lots of bowls and plates clean and ready to go because people will bring bags of chips and tubs of guacamole that will be begging for immediate homes. And no one should feel that his or her contribution is overlooked, be it materials, food, or just his or her own delightful presence. The most important thing you can do at Crafternoon is make your guests feel warm and welcome.

BREAKING THE ICE! A HOW-TO ON HOW TO STRIKE UP A CONVERSATION AND KEEP IT BURNING BRIGHTLY

You are the host or hostess of your very own Crafternoon. You want it to be a great success, but how do you pull it off? You've got friends in low places, and high ones, too, and Crafternoon is going to bring them together, but *you'll* have to keep them from falling apart. Here are some general how-tos from me, your Crafternoon Cruise Director:

As the host, try to connect your friends by their common interests. If you have a friend who totally loves the Yankees and a friend who totally loves the Mets, they could talk about baseball! Oh, but they might get into and argument . . . never mind. Okay, try to find a common interest that your friends will agree on, and introduce them with a simple, "So-and-so, this is what's-her-name. You guys both grew up in Virginia!" and then walk away. Leave them to turn the small talk into a conversation.

When I first began hosting Crafternoon, I always made name tags for all of my attendees. I know that might sound kind of lame and corporate-cocktail-partyesque to some folks, but it worked like a charm. How many times have you been introduced to someone at a party and then five seconds later SHAZAM—his name disappears from your brain. You ask him again and struggle to get a firmer brain grip on that name, repeating it aloud as the experts tell you to, trying your best to make that name stick in your mental library. And then a new person comes along with a new name and SHAZAM—the first name disappears again. But if everyone is wearing a name tag, you can just refer back to that every time you forget. Maybe it's because I'm a visual learner, but I can assure you that my retention rate on names significantly increases when people are wearing name tags. I forgot to purchase name tags for my last few Crafternoons, and while I still remember the faces of the newbies, I forgot the names. I hate to think I'll run into them someday and know who they are but forget what to call them. And name tags come in especially handy when that friend of a friend's boyfriend shows up. You've met him at least ten times but you cannot, for the life of you, remember his name. Is it Ben or Jeremy? What if his name is Ben and her ex-boyfriend's name is Jeremy and he resents you for calling him her ex-boyfriend's name? Name tags eliminate all of these problems. And besides, they give folks something to personalize, and that is another good conversation sparker.

If you are the guest at a Crafternoon where you don't know a lot of folks, be prepared to be friendly. I realize it can be hard to be the perky, friendly stranger in a room filled with folks who are all BFFs, but sometimes it's the only way to roll. Get out there and get outgoing and you'll make some new friends in no time. It can help if you wear something unusual in this sort of situation. Not something crazy, like a spacesuit, but something that is visually interesting; you know, the kind of things that they refer to on those home-shopping shows as "conversation pieces." I'm not saying you should be covered in head-to-toe cubic zirconium, but something slightly eye-catching will give fellow partiers something to talk to you about. So if you're attending a new Crafternoon, why not wear something you've crafted yourself? I guarantee the conversations will start flowing. A handknit necklace is sure to elicit questions about technique, materials, your craft history, and so on. And then you're on the path to Conversationland.

CRAFT OUTSIDE THE BOX

While I've given you loads of projects to get your Crafternoons going, you don't have to stop there. Maybe there are certain elements of a project that I've suggested that you're not stoked about. Say, for instance, you're psyched to start knitting, but you have a deep and inexplicable fear of yarn. Don't give up on knitting altogether! You could knit with ribbons or rope or shoelaces or wet spaghetti instead. Don't let things become stumbling blocks—find work-arounds. Granted, there are some things that cannot be worked around, like needing a super-hot flame to make your own iron sword. I saw that on PBS, and the flame seemed pretty necessary. But sword making aside, a lot of crafts have elements that are open to modification, if you can just open your mind. Crafting is such a satisfying occupation because it stimulates your mind at the same time that it activates your hands. Remember Jazz Hands from Intro to Modern Jazz Dance? Well, you've got Craft Hands. And they are directly linked to your smart, smart brain. So use those hands and that mind of yours to find solutions to your craft problems.

Why not blindly follow the instructions laid out in front of you, you may ask? Because that's just not terribly interesting. If you want some easy-peasy, paint-by-the-numbers craft kit, then buy a paint-by-the-numbers craft kit. But you'll be missing out on one of the great joys of crafting—problem solving! Problem solving is the Fountain of Youth. All those crosswords and Sudoku puzzles and *Jeopardy!* viewings are ways of keeping the mind engaged. And when you discover a new way to tackle something, it feels like you're discovering a whole new world. So fear not—you'll find your way around this brave new craft. Just be willing to imagine that the crafting world might not be as flat as it first seemed. And certainly not as full of prestamped, precut tiger-face latch-hook kits as you first imagined.

WE DON'T NEED NO EDUCATION . . . OR DO WE?

If this book is doing its job, it's helped you figure out how to tackle a new craft without necessarily having an expert in the room. But as a person who learns in a variety of ways, I find that the assistance of a good instructor is incredibly helpful, no matter how awesome your resource guide may be. Sometimes you'll discover a craft that you want to learn, but you can't think of anyone who can teach you. You may want to try your nimble hand at the art of underwater basket weaving, but your circle of Crafternoon friends lacks an underwater-basket-weaving guru. Armed with some well-researched instructions and some tenacity, you should be able to get pretty far. But you may just *want* to take a class. Nothing to be ashamed of there—continuing education is a beautiful thing. If you've already made some headway with your self-taught stylings, the things you learn in class will be icing on your knowledge cake. And they will probably provide the filling between the layers, too. Plus, you might make some cool, crafty new friends in class whom you can invite to your next Crafternoon. So remember this: *You* don't have to be the expert every time! Find someone who can teach you the ways of creweling or bejeweling and enjoy the learning time.

ADVENTURES IN RESEARCH!

While there are so many wonderful resources for craft ideas (hello, you're reading one of them!), one should never underestimate the power of research. While I was working on this compendium of craftiness, I visited my college for a few days of R&R. Actually, it was more like a few days of R & R & W & R—Rest, Relaxation, Writing, and Research! I holed up for two beautiful days in the library, where I was surrounded by endless sources of inspiration. My alma mater has an amazing library filled with books on every possible subject, and I was thrilled to find a plethora of books on crafts. So whenever I was hit with a bit of writer's block, I'd get up and get researching. It would have taken me months to get through all of the books that interested me, but a few volumes really stood out. I think my favorite was a slim 125-year-old tome called *Home Occupations* by Janet E. Ruutz-Rees. A part of the series of Appleton's Home Books, it was published in 1882 by D. Appleton and Company. In her introduction, Ms. Ruutz-Rees acknowledges that her readers have a lot of time on their hands, and they've got to do something with all of that spare time. The goal of her book was to offer projects that match the following criteria: "More satisfactory than the mere exciting chase of amusement, and less irksome than the monotonous pursuit of compulsory employment."

I couldn't have said it better myself. Ms. Ruutz-Rees then kicks off the book with a compelling chapter, "Showing What Can Be Done with Leather," where she explains things like "the easiest thing for a beginner to attempt in leather is to copy a spray of ivy." Hmm, copying a spray of ivy in leather seems pretty difficult to me. Perhaps this book is proof of how greatly times have changed. Maybe in 1882, just about anyone could figure out how to make a spray of ivy out of leather. People of that era had more manual dexterity, or maybe they just spent more time with ivy. Or maybe the book is proof that crafting is completely subjective. Ms. Ruutz-Rees thought making an ivy leaf out of leather was a breeze, but to me, and maybe to some of her brethren, anything that involves the use of "a small brad-awl" sounds incredibly intimidating. The book's other chapters cover such topics as "The Possibilities of Tissue Paper," "The Uses of Card-Board," and "Modeling in Wax—Fruit, Vegetables." She even suggests straw plaiting as a fun activity. According to her directions, after plaiting one need merely bring it to a milliner's to be pressed and shaped and, voilà—you've got a hot new bonnet.

While I skipped past some of the above-mentioned topics, I really enjoyed skimming the pages for new ideas. And I do like the notion of "rustic-work," something else J. R. R. recommends. I'm not entirely clear on what that is, but it involves things found in the woods. And that sounds pretty exciting. Now I just have to do a little more research. See how that goes? You do some research, and it makes you want to do more research. And that research leads you to more research . . . you can see why PhDs take so darn long to achieve. And if you find your project mapped out in a kids' craft book, don't feel as though you're too old to tackle it—that just means you and your friends will probably be able to manage it.

CRAFTERNOON RESOURCE NOOK

If you want to get some in-depth crafty advice in real time from real, live crafters, why not throw your question out to the World Wide Web? The CrafterNation keeps in touch at www.crafternoon.com. Check back regularly for tips, photos, links, blogs, songs, and videos about Crafternoons and crafters across the nation and the world. And add your own info while you're there. That's the beauty of the World Wide Web—ideas and events are instantaneously shared, and inspiration lurks around every corner. There are many crafty people who enjoy sharing advice and anecdotes on message boards. Don't believe me? Type the word "crafts" into a search engine and see what you come up with. Sure, you might stumble across some witchcraft sites, but you'll find some great craft sites as well. Look for the message boards and read some of the question-and-answer threads. If you think the responses reflect some expertise, toss your question onto the board and see what happens!

My point is this: Reading exposes us to new ideas, and new ideas are what keep Crafternoon alive. You know what else exposes you to new ideas? Going to new places and trying new things. Heck, if I get my hands on some fresh straw, I am going to try plaiting it. And once I plait it, I'm going to hit the yellow pages and find the nearest milliner. And I will ask that milliner to shape my plaits into a lovely little bonnet. It may have been a while since he or she had a request like that, but I bet that milliner will be pretty excited to see me.

IN CRAFTY CONCLUSION

I'm afraid that we have come to the end, my crafty friends. We've pasted, purled, and partied our way through a year of Crafternoons. Now we are all part of the same great crafting community, a place that lives inside and outside of ourselves, a place of inspiration and aspirations. So craft on, my Crafternooners! Bring the message of good times, great friends, and constant creativity to your family, your friends, and everyone beyond that. We can craft ourselves a world that's filled with hope and caring, a place that we are proud to call our own. I want the world to rise up and laugh and craft and care about each other. And though I'm sad to see you go, I know we'll meet again some Crafternoon. Parting is such sweet sorrow, so let's have Crafternoons on every tomorrow!

HANDY-DANDY, AT-A-GLANCE CRAFT-SUPPLY LISTS

You're gathering your craft supplies, but you're feeling a tad lazy. Use this list as a fast reference for all of your Crafternoon needs. For more details, refer back to the helpful instructions in each chapter.

JANUARY:
Knotty or Nice
Rope
Scissors

OPTIONAL
Cork
Jewelry wire
Jewelry pliers
Scarves

FEBRUARY:
Love in the Crafternoon

Fabric
Ribbon
Heart-shaped cookie cutter
Pins
Cotton stuffing or fiberfill
Thread
Needle
Scissors
Boxes
Paint
Medium-size paintbrushes
Magazines or other paper images
Decoupage medium
White glue
Underwear
Puffy paint or fabric pens
Construction paper
Glue sticks

OPTIONAL
Chopsticks
Dried herbs

MARCH:
Charitable Crafternoon
Yarn
Knitting needles
Yarn needles
Vases or jars
Flowers
Scissors
Construction paper
Glue

OPTIONAL
Tissue paper
Ribbons

APRIL:
Paperwork! (a.k.a. Quilling with My Homies and Papermaking)
Paper
Glue
Toothpicks or nails or quills
Tweezers
Posterboard
Colored pens or pencils
Scrap paper
Water
Scissors or X-Acto blade
Blender
Screen
Basin or tub

OPTIONAL
Felt or chamois cloth
Rolling pin
Pressed flowers
Shiny paper
Glitter
Dye

MAY:
Jewelry-Making Madness
Ribbons
Pendants
Sculpey clay
Water-based acrylic paint
Small paintbrushes
Shrinky Dinks plastic
Brooch pins
Strong glue
Oven
Scissors
X-Acto blade
Colored pencils
Cord

OPTIONAL
Necklace closure or craft wire

JUNE:
Nothing but Needlepoint
Canvas (10 or 12 count)
Ribbon
Yarn
Yarn needles
Sewing needle
Thread
Graph paper
Colored pencils
T-shirts
Embroidery floss
Embroidery needles
Scissors
Cloth napkins
Fabric pen or ballpoint

OPTIONAL

Fabric pens and pencils

Embroidery hoop

JULY:
Freedom Craft!

ALL SUPPLIES ARE OPTIONAL.
FEEL THE FREEDOM!

Felt

Thread

Needles

Straight pins

Scissors

A book

Leaves or flowers

Construction paper or posterboard

Old magazines

Old books

Old newspapers

Glue sticks

Contact paper

Magnetic sheets or magnetic tape

OPTIONAL

Chopsticks

AUGUST:
When a Problem Comes Around, You Must Quilt It!

Graph paper

Pencil

Ruler

Template plastic

Scissors (for cutting plastic and fabric)

Fabric

Sewing needle

Thread

Batting

Quilting hoop

Thimble

Wide satin ribbon

Hera marker

Straight pins

Craft pliers

Head pins

Fishhook earrings

OPTIONAL

Chopstick or knitting needle

SEPTEMBER:
ClayNation

Sculpey or Super Sculpey clay

Water-based acrylic paint

Paintbrushes

Oven

Fimo clay

Kabob stick or chopstick

Baking sheet

Craft wire

OCTOBER:
Costume-Making Cavalcade and Homespun-Attire Extravaganza

Newspaper

Flour

Water

Balloons

Basin

Paints

Paintbrushes

X-Acto blade

Elastic

Kraft paper (butcher paper)

Pencil

Fabric

Scissors

Sewing machine or hand-sewing needle

Thread

Straight pins

Sculpey clay

Oven

Black and white water-based acrylic paint

Ruler

OPTIONAL

Aluminum foil

Tissue paper

Construction paper

Glue

NOVEMBER:
Knitting Know-How

Yarn

Knitting needles

Yarn needle

Scissors

OPTIONAL

Adornments such as buttons, baubles, bows, and beads

DECEMBER:
Harbingers of the Holidays

Kraft paper (butcher paper)

Styrofoam trays

Chopstick or pencil

Sponges

Water-based acrylic paints

Mini bagels

Red and green felt-tip pens

Clear nail polish

Ribbon

Glue

Scissors

Scrap paper

Wooden clothespins

Fabric scraps

Ribbon

Paintbrushes

Fimo clay

Carving implement

Oven